TONI CAVELTI

TONI CAVELTI

A Jeweller's Life

Max Wyman

Foreword by Bill Reid

Douglas & McIntyre

Vancouver/Toronto

Douglas & McIntyre Ltd.
1615 Venables Street
Vancouver, British Columbia V5L 2H1

Canadian Cataloguing in Publication Data

Wyman, Max, 1939-
Toni Cavelti

ISBN 1-55054-526-4

1. Cavelti, Toni. 2. Jewelers—British Columbia—Biography. 3. Jewelry trade—British
Columbia. 4. British Columbia—Biography. I. Title.
NK7398.C38W95 1996   739.27'092   c96-910288-7

Editing by Saeko Usukawa
Design by George Vaitkunas
Front cover photograph by Hans Sipma: brooch, 18-carat gold, pure gold dust, platinum,
   diamonds, 40 mm x 50 mm, 1960
Back cover photograph by Hans Sipma: brooch-pendant, 18-carat gold, platinum,
   diamonds, 40 mm x 70 mm, circa 1988
Colour photographs on pages vi, 2 and 62 to 178 by Hans Sipma
Black-and-white photographs on pages ii, 7, 13 and 15 by Selwyn Pullan
Family photographs courtesy of the Cavelti family
Printed and bound in Canada by Hemlock Printers Ltd.
Printed on acid-free paper

Page ii:
The process of creating a drop earring: lightly domed and textured gold sections are
placed in plasticine, where they will be encased in plaster and soldered together. After
the solder has cooled, the plaster and plasticine will be removed, leaving a perfect join.

Contents

Foreword

A multistrand *collier* of fresh-water pearls with 18-carat gold and diamond clasp; mabe pearl earrings; a combined brooch and pearl enhancer with an Australian opal and diamonds.

One basic quality unites all of the works of mankind that speak to us in human, recognizable voices across the barriers of time, culture and space: the simple quality of being well-made. Of course, it doesn't start or end there. It is the elegant line, the subtle curve, the sure precise brush stroke, that moves or excites us; but without that mastery of technique, the message is so poor in the shades of meaning that constitute human communication that it becomes meaningless.

In a world where we more and more seek out and admire finely crafted objects, we less and less know how to make them. The old, infinitely precious web that carried the hard-won skills from one generation of artisans to the next, that provided the visual and tactile language by which the artists of every age could give expression to their times and themselves, has become, in our time, as thin and frayed as our hope of heaven. It may be, as some say, that new skills and other means will give rise to other equally valid expressions; but this does not diminish the loss of what was for so many millennia an essential part of our humanity. So it makes even more important the occasional bright segments of that web which still retain their strength and elegance.

One of these was, and even more today is, the preserve of Toni Cavelti. Toni is a virtuoso of only one trade; but what a trade it is. Validated by an existence almost as long as the human past of our time on earth—one of the great dynamic forces of history, a set of skills so difficult to master that anything subsequently learned seems simple: the old, magical, devious, constantly expanding bag of tricks of the goldsmith.

Toni arrived in Vancouver in the early fifties with eight dollars in his pocket, a knowledge of three languages—none of which was English—a box that contained his tools, and the seed that over the years has produced the thousands of glittering objects which have done much to brighten the local scene as well as find recognition abroad.

I invite you to enjoy his creations, to cherish them as beautiful objects, and to love them because they represent part of the process that began a long time ago, and with a little luck and a few more like Toni Cavelti, may continue for a long time yet.

Bill Reid

Introduction

Before starting the preparation of this book, I took some time to read publications by and about other jewellers, most of them internationally known. I soon came to understand that these jewellers all offered something quite special. In most cases, their jewellery was often very costly, using extremely rare and valuable gemstones in items created for a wealthy and often famous international *clientèle*. What was also notable was that these jewellers were able—through location and heritage—to evolve their own unique design styles, some of them inspired by the work of designers of centuries past, some who created their own patterns that became their trademark designs.

None of that can be said of the items shown in this book. What is represented here is a goldsmith's work over half a century, work that was often influenced by the requirements of economics, location and demand. More often than not, the jewellery represented here was created for a particular person for a particular event, often on a strict (though not necessarily low) budget. It was also created in a city in which, when I arrived in 1954, the concept of the independent jewellery designer-cum-goldsmith was barely understood, and in which, as a result, the product's appearance was sometimes dictated by the need for business survival.

What this book shows is the product of one jeweller's workshop, though as work on the book progressed, I realized that it was going to be impossible to show all the pieces that deserved display. Some of them I had simply forgotten (in the early years, my design records were far from perfect); others I had lost sight of; yet others came to mind too late to be included. However, I wish to express my lasting gratitude to all the individuals who, over the years, have had a part in the creation and enjoyment of the products of this workshop.

In terms of inspiration, the continuing exploration of new forms of artistic expression by painters, sculptors, architects and fashion designers (many of them my friends) has greatly influenced my designs. In terms of physical fabrication, while everything shown here was my own imaginative creation, I have often been aided in the manufacture by a number of skilled and dedicated craftspeople, in particular Peter Bruderer, who was for many years my most committed and trusted shop foreman; Alois Lander and Rudi Suter, whose technical skills and fresh approach to jewellery design left a very positive mark; and my present craftsmen, all of whom have been with me for over ten years: Perry Serron, Patrick Casanova, Bruce Wilson and Bryan Taylor. I have been fortunate to have the help of an imaginative and loyal sales and office staff. Not least, I am grateful for the enthusiasm and support of my customers, many of whom, I am proud to say, have become personal friends.

It is to those numerous individuals who have been a part of these fifty years as a jeweller, and above all to my wife, Hildegard, without whose unstinting love and understanding support I could never have managed to do what I have done, that this book is dedicated.

Toni Cavelti

TONI CAVELTI

A Jeweller's Life

Strands of 18-carat gold fashioned into drop earrings; ear-clips with *pavé*-set diamonds; a bangle bracelet of sculpted 18-carat gold with *pavé*-set diamonds; a ring made of 18-carat gold.

Two sets of glass doors guard Toni Cavelti's jewellery salon on West Georgia Street in downtown Vancouver. You open the first yourself; as you pass through, the internal set glides open, then slips silently back into place behind you. The honks and voices of the street give way to a velvet hush, and you find yourself in a discreetly illuminated haven.

This is the home of a craft as ancient as known civilization. Here, beneath a pear-shaped crystal chandelier, you may inspect and acquire objects that give tangible form both to the human individual's yearning to adorn itself with beauty, and to the parallel human urge to lay claims of ownership to the uncommon.

Gold, diamonds, precious stones—they have been coveted for their rarity, their beauty and for the value bestowed on them since the ancient Egyptians made their first gold ornaments 5,000 years ago. The Egyptians buried some of the most beautiful and sophisticated products of their goldsmiths and jewellers in the tombs of their kings. The nomad Scythian warriors who roamed the Russian steppes 2,500 years ago carried large amounts of gold, as ornaments and as weapons; when a chief died, his gold was buried with him, along with animals and human sacrifices. Gold was one of the three gifts the Magi brought. Old wives said you could cure a sty on the eye by rubbing it with a gold ring, and Chaucer mentioned the medicinal properties of potable gold.

The story of the role played by gold in the evolution of civilized society brings together the best and the worst of the human individual: reverence and greed—the instinctive exaltation of the exquisite, the fierce and unquenchable urge for possession. Gold, as Shakespeare's Romeo knew, could seduce a saint. Many men have died following Virgil's "accurst craving for gold." Many others have tried in vain to manufacture it. The potions and spells of the alchemists from ancient China to medieval Europe who searched for the magical substance that would transmute base metals into gold provided the foundations for much of modern chemistry.

But it is not only gold that excites. We know that gemstones are merely mineral fragments—carbon (diamond), aluminum oxide (ruby, sapphire), beryllium-aluminum silicate (emerald), borosilicate (tourmaline), aluminosilicate (topaz), silicon dioxide (amethyst)—but they too have become, as much as gold, talismanic objects. Forged in the hot crucible of earth's creation, yielded reluctantly by stubborn granites, gemstones seduce the eye, gladden the heart or (encrusted on crowns and thrones and priestly capes) inspire respect and impress the multitudes. We have pinned to them oracular significance—a stone for every birth sign, and a stone for every need and hope: ruby for passion, sapphire for chastity, amethyst to keep you sober, diamonds a girl's best friend. Gemstones are cut, rounded, faceted and polished into an endless, dancing flirtation with light: the exuberant diamond refracting whole light into flashes of pure and thrilling colour, the star sapphire throwing off its sparkling six-rayed asterisms, the shy gold-green chrysoberyl yielding its beauty in a single cat's-eye ray.

Though the lustrous objects laid out with spare care in Toni Cavelti's salon have been fashioned by hands and eyes informed by today's sophisticated tastes and fashions, they are freighted with the human clamour of the centuries. Here, in this ring or that brooch, may be traces of the beaten gold that decorated the poop of Cleopatra's barge, of a sliver pared by a cutpurse from the unmilled rim of a medieval coin, of an ancient amulet fashioned to protect a Greek warrior. As the part-Haida jeweller and sculptor Bill Reid once put it, "Every time the vandals melt down the shiny baubles of our past, the goldsmith puts them together again in a different form."

None of this is voiced when we step into Toni Cavelti's discreet salon, or perhaps even thought about. We have other things to concern us: the sleek and scintillant products created by one of the last of a fast-disappearing kind, the independent artist/craftsman jeweller.

Toni Cavelti has spent fifty years perfecting his mastery of a difficult, demanding and ancient craft whose origins date back at least to Sumerian times and whose techniques have remained largely unaltered down the centuries. It is a craft to whose mastery there are no shortcuts. It demands its practitioner be a pragmatic visionary: a person whose talents embrace both the technical and the creative. Sculpture makes similar demands in some respects, but it is not necessary for a sculptor to become an expert at a dozen or more different techniques: casting, soldering, drilling, embossing, chasing and

One of the most demanding tasks for a diamond setter preparing a *pavé* finish is the fashioning of perfect "seats" (the spaces into which the diamonds are set) and "beads" (the tiny round clasps made by cutting slivers of the gold or platinum frame to hold the diamonds in place).

engraving, construction, wirework, *repoussé* (in which a surface is ornamented with designs in relief hammered out from the back by hand), granulation (a tricky means of surface texturing involving tiny beads of gold, perfected by the Etruscans), and the charming old technique of *couper à-jour* (the daylight cut, not much seen now, but still at Cavelti's fingertips—a method of opening up the back of the rounded holes in a setting to allow extra light to enhance the stone's charms).

Cavelti's early years of apprenticeship in Switzerland instilled in him a sense of purpose that has never left him, though it might be somewhat unfashionable now: a sense of himself as an individual both privileged (by his training) and obliged (by his talents) to create objects of intrinsic beauty, value and permanence. But to carry out this craft well, with pride, as Cavelti does, is not only demanding, it is time-consuming and expensive to the point of economic uncompetitiveness.

It is, as much as anything, a matter of man versus machine. With the introduction of mass-production methods at the time of the Industrial Revolution, the goldsmith became a businessman, hiring craftsmen and designers to help meet increased demand from increasingly affluent customers. In the late nineteenth century, the great Peter Carl Fabergé was working for a *clientèle*, primarily the Russian nobility, to whom money was no object. When he received a commission—for one of his legendary decorated eggs, perhaps—he could call on the talents of a vast workshop of specialist craftsmen: some who were skilled at engraving, some who were experts in enamelling, one who knew all about figurines, one who was good at damascening (in which threads of gold or silver are inlaid in another metal to form contrasting

patterns), one who knew how to construct the gold lions that would make the whole elaborate work stand up. Perhaps as many as twenty people worked for two or three months on a single precious object.

Inevitably, as mass-production techniques took over, the quality dropped. It was a determination to restore the significance of the individual goldsmith-jeweller as dedicated craftsman/artist that inspired the late nineteenth-century Arts and Crafts movement, with its emphasis on the honest, well-made object. A commitment to those traditional principles has always driven Cavelti. But he believes he is part of the last generation to be able to maintain the quality and singularity that is found in this salon. The golden age of the Fabergés and Cellinis doesn't exist any more, and isn't likely to again.

Cavelti has seen pieces carrying designer names that his clients, accustomed to the quality of his workshop, would sniff at and turn down. What makes it possible for big names to sell mediocre jewellery is customer ignorance. Few of us have a very sophisticated knowledge of gold or jewellery, so the safest thing is to go to a name, someone whose advertisement we've seen in *Vogue* or an in-flight duty-free brochure: the comfort of the known. And meanwhile, the master craftsman, working on a one-to-one basis, continues to struggle. He will always have a niche, but that niche is daily becoming smaller. We live in the pared-down, fiscally responsible 1990s; fewer and fewer people are spending large amounts of money on objects they don't strictly need. There is less and less room for someone like Cavelti, offering one-of-a-kind creations of unusual design and beauty.

There is also the problem of manufacturing expense. Cavelti acknowledges that it would be cheaper, and perhaps more efficient, to contract out his work to, say, manufacturers in Thailand, where labour costs are a tenth of what they are in North America. In the mid-1980s, he considered it as a serious possibility: take a design or a model abroad and order perhaps fifty copies. But he has always resisted the temptation. It would, in his view, be cheating. People come to his store because they assume they can buy a piece of jewellery designed by Toni Cavelti and manufactured either by him or under his close personal supervision. They also come to him because they know that each item he has to offer is unique. How would Mr. Jones feel if, after buying a brooch for his wife one Christmas, he returned for something else for her birthday and found the identical brooch in the showcase? Toni Cavelti shakes his head and frowns. It would be a significant disappointment to the customer.

Respect for the customer is pre-eminent (a man of unfailing old-world courtesy, Cavelti will never appear behind his counter without a jacket and tie—or, in the days when he worked on the bench, his white coat: customers used to call him Dr. Casey) and discretion is automatic (the gentleman shopping for gifts for both his wife and his mistress at Christmas will never have to fear that the boxes will be confused).

All this probably makes him an anachronism in an increasingly fast-paced, mechanized world. He has never done any of the things that conventional business wisdom dictates; he has never had a sale, never offered discounts on his merchandise. Each item in his inventory is priced when it is made, and that's the price he sticks to, though that doesn't stop people from trying to bargain. One of his least favourite customers is the individual who waves a bundle of cash and offers half the asking price, expecting to be met halfway; particularly in the early years, attempts to haggle a price down would drive him to distraction.

Cavelti has acquired, over the years, a rich understanding of human nature. The desire for acquisition can lay the human soul naked, and—part diplomat, part psychologist—he goes out of his way to read people's minds, make them feel comfortable, give them what they come to him for. His is a business that demands a high degree of sensitivity to the balance between customer desires and customer ability to pay.

Getting up from his workbench, flecks of gold in his eyebrows, jeweller's rouge on his hands, tip of a fingernail half filed off, to sell a young couple their modest first engagement ring always gave him as much satisfaction as the big-ticket sales. He takes pride and pleasure in cultivating customer relationships. He recalls, for instance, the man who brought in an emerald ring he had bought in Brazil. "How much do you think it's worth?" the man asked. Cavelti showed the man an emerald ring of his own. "That's obviously much better, and more expensive," said the man. Cavelti agreed that his was a better ring—though it turned out that Cavelti was charging several thousand dollars less for his ring than the visitor had paid for his. The man bought Cavelti's ring on the spot, sent the other back to Brazil for a refund, and became one of Cavelti's most loyal customers, ordering hundreds of thousands of dollars' worth of jewellery over the years—and never once asking "How much?" again.

In the early years, when he was developing his business, Toni Cavelti travelled the world in search of precious stones—Thailand for rubies and sapphires, Brazil for tourmalines and aquamarines, Antwerp for diamonds. But although travelling to buy gems can be a delightful adventure, it is fraught with pitfalls. You're in a different culture, you don't speak the language, you're under time pressure, you're at the mercy of dealers whose only object is to take as much money from you as possible. Perhaps most important of all, in a business which is all to do with reflected and refracted light, you're assessing stones according to the local conditions, not according to the light that you're familiar with. Several times, says Cavelti, "I have come back with an item that I have paid a pretty good price for, and I take it out when I get home and look at it under my own light and know that I would never have bought it at any price if it had been offered to me in Vancouver."

Today, he works primarily with a network of gem dealers in Canada, most of them subsidiaries of the leading London and European dealers. They send him stones on approval; he examines them at his leisure, in his own light, and buys only what he wants. The system means that he probably pays ten per cent more for stones than he would if he travelled; set against that are the savings in travel costs, the ability to take his time over his choices, and the knowledge that he can trust the people he deals with.

These are important considerations, particularly since Cavelti has always insisted that (direct commissions apart) he will take full personal responsibility for buying a stone. No likelihood here that he'll approach a customer and suggest he or she should buy a $50,000 stone he has just spotted; he'd be embarrassed by that. Instead, he puts his own cash on the line, buys the stone, sets it—*then* shows it to the chosen customer. Yes, he admits, he occasionally makes mistakes. But only occasionally. Experience has shown him how to gauge which customers will like what. Native Swiss pragmatism, too. "I'm not the kind of artist to want to live in humble surroundings," he once said, "just so I could make something that no one liked. I wouldn't do that."

His own favourite stone? "An emerald," he says. "A fine

emerald is very beautiful." But then he adds: "I like sapphires, maybe because they are available in high quality still. Rubies, too, though they are almost impossible to find in any size now. And certainly there's absolutely nothing wrong with a well-cut, beautiful diamond."

Two floors above the quiet salon is the airy, brightly lit workshop in which these burnished masterpieces are created. Here is where the patient, industrious business of crafting takes place—stretching and thinning, cutting and shaping, casting and beating, filing and bending, chipping and clipping, setting and soldering, turning and polishing. Here, raw metal and gemstones are transformed, not by any alchemist's magic but by fire and muscle and painstaking skill, into objects of beauty and desire. Here is where Cavelti and his associates create sculpture to wear.

Like any craftsperson's workplace, this linked set of rooms has a functional, purposeful air. People sit at orderly rows of benches built to principles of user-friendly design ergonomics that date from centuries before the concept was invented. The main working platform of each bench is a rectangular table set at approximately the height of the middle of the seated worker's upper arm. This table bears much of the impedimenta of the goldsmith—hammers, files, saws, bodkins on which work in progress can be firmly clasped. Here are small envelopes and wide-mouthed trays of precious stones; slips of paper bearing sketched designs; part-finished items of jewellery—half a bangle, an earclip, a diamond-encrusted bracelet gaping with holes for those scattered rubies, still to be set. Clipped vertically to the table's right edge, within easy reach of the worker, is the slim tubing of a blowtorch, a small flame almost invisibly alight at the upper, elbowed end, ready to blast heat at the turn of a knob.

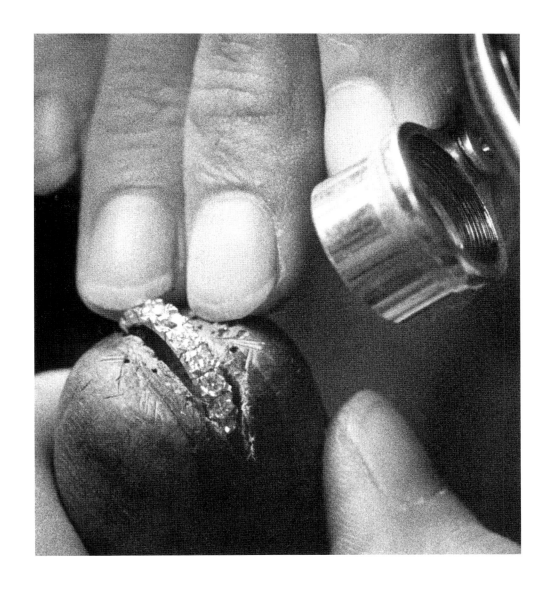

Into this worktop is cut a wide semicircle, from the centre of which protrudes the jeweller's pin—a broad peg of hard Indian oak against which much of the necessary filing and hammering and nailing is done. They last two years, maybe three, these pins; constant wear makes them look like battered pieces of brittle old sponge. The indentation of the curve embraces the craftsman within his work, yet allows him free movement of his arms around the pin.

Below the pin sits a small, retractable tray bearing the blocks of material on which the metals are heated: Indian charcoal for gold (the charcoal absorbs and reflects the applied heat, giving an even temperature to both the upper and lower sides of the object being worked) and a thick ceramic plate for substances that can take more heat, such as platinum.

Beside these pads sit small trays of gold solder. The secret behind a seamless gold join lies in the solder; it must be of a slightly lower carat value than the gold of the object itself, so that it will melt sooner, but it must be as close a colour match as possible in order not to look obtrusive and out of place. Solder can be bought in varying degrees of hardness, though Cavelti's craftsmen prefer to create their own, adding only the slightest amount of alloy to their standard 18-carat base so that the colour difference is imperceptible once the solder has hardened. The richness of colour and massy texture of 18-carat gold is a Cavelti trademark. Production-line jewellers will use gold as low in purity as 10 carats, arguing that it is preferable for its hardness. Cavelti has always scorned that argument, and remains a stickler for the precise 18-carat value, though under international tolerance limits it would be perfectly legal for him to shave off a couple of tenths of a carat and still stamp it as 18 carats: many manufacturers do, particularly those involved in mass-market jewellery, where the economy can result in extra profits of tens of thousands of dollars.

Below the tray on which the heating is done is a second, slightly inset work platform; here lie more tools, more materials, and here is where the filings fall as work progresses against the hardwood pin. The filings, be assured, are not ignored. Filings, floor-sweepings, old brushes, polishing compounds—they are all carefully collected and once a year are sent off to the supplier's refinery, where the mixture is consigned to the fire and pure gold, platinum and silver are re-extracted.

Across the room from the workbenches are the foundry rooms where the various casting processes take place. For one-of-a-kind items, Cavelti favours the *cire perdue*, or lost wax, process. A precisely carved wax model is invested in plaster, which is dried (usually overnight) and placed in an oven to burn out the wax. It is then placed on a centrifuge, where gold is "shot" into the void left by the burned-out wax. When the casting has cooled, the plaster is removed, leaving the gold form.

For a casting that is likely to be part of a series (a leaf motif, perhaps), a model is made in metal (gold, silver or brass), and heated rubber is applied to the model under pressure to create a mould. When it is cold and dry, this mould is cut open, the model is removed, and hot wax is inserted to create a cast. This can be repeated indefinitely, with each wax casting being subjected to the *cire perdue* process described above.

In these foundry rooms, the harnessed forces of steam, vacuum and fire bear hissing witness to the elemental origins of the goldsmith's art.

Fire is the constant companion of any new piece of jewellery in the making, from the heating and pouring of the raw ingot through annealing and to the final assembly by soldering.

Anton (Toni) Cavelti was born on June 13, 1931, in Ilanz, a community of about 800, high in the Rumantsch-speaking canton of les Grisons (Graubünden) on the borders of Italy and Austria in the Eastern Swiss Alps. Not far away is the source of the Rhine river; Ilanz calls itself "the first city on the Rhine." Its ceremonial crest, displayed proudly above the railway station, bears a crown with a river running through it.

He was the eighth of ten children, and the youngest of five boys. The year he was born, his father, a deeply religious man, was chosen to play Christ in an Ilanz production of an Oberammergau-style passion play. All summer long his father died nightly on the cross.

Cavelti's father, Gion-Mathias Cavelti, was the only son (in a family of seven children) of a prosperous cabinetmaker and land-owning dignitary in the nearby village of Sagogn. Gion-Mathias had taken his university education and been trained as a teacher in the Grisons capital of Chur. Cavelti's mother, Maria-Onna Neuwirth, the eldest of fourteen children, was a home economics teacher from Sevgein, another village close by. They were married in 1920. On the day of their marriage, Gion-Mathias confessed to his bride that he had resigned from his teaching post to run for the office of president (or mayor) of Sagogn. She was heartbroken. Her dream had been to marry the schoolmaster and settle down to a happy, quiet life raising a family. The pressures of public office seemed daunting by comparison.

But Gion-Mathias was not to be deterred. The handsome, articulate university graduate, already a popular figure in the village, won the post with ease. He took the position seriously, and his son says villagers still talk about the way Gion-Mathias brought running water to Sagogn—no small task in 1920s Switzerland. However, it was an ill-paying job, and as the family slowly grew, the financial pressures intensified. Gion-Mathias accepted his father's help in establishing an *usteria*, a small, publike inn catering to locals and occasional travellers, but he was unsuited to the enterprise. Small talk was not his *forte*, and he did not mix well with his customers, mostly local farmers, small tradespeople and labourers.

By the time Toni was born, the family had moved to a four-hundred-year-old stone house in Ilanz, where Gion-Mathias had taken the post of official in charge of bankruptcies. The compassionate Cavelti had a keen personal understanding of the severity of life in those Depression years, and rather than force people into bankruptcy, he would do what he could to defer payments and help them out. Unfortunately, by 1938, in the face of the heavy financial demands of his family (now numbering ten children ranging in age from seventeen years to four), Gion-Mathias found himself in a similar position of insolvency.

Maria-Onna Neuwirth and Gion-Mathias Cavelti, 1920.

Toni's mother, doing what she could to bolster the family's income, fell back on her home economics training to run a fabric and clothing store from a tiny counter on the main floor of the family home. Cavelti remembers going from door to door as her bag-carrier in the mountain villages, standing quietly by as she busily unrolled bolts of cloth on the kitchen tables, draped fabric over the shoulders of the farmers' wives and daughters, pointed out fashions in the latest magazines. Usually, her customers paid in farm produce: fruit, preserves, bread, meat, once a live rooster.

For a man of Gion-Mathias's stature, the situation was intolerable. To support his family, he took a position as a travelling insurance salesman, covering a wide area of eastern Switzerland. One trip took him to Sankt Gallen, or St. Gallen, the capital city of the German-speaking canton of St. Gallen, located ten kilometres from Lake Constance, which separates Germany from northeast Switzerland. Here he befriended a family who convinced him that St. Gallen, with its superior schooling and trade training, was a far more suitable place to raise his children. Within a matter of months, he loaded the entire family and its remaining possessions onto a moving company's truck—boys seated on a mattress propped against the raised tailgate—and headed north to St. Gallen and a new life.

The distance from Ilanz to St. Gallen is less than 100 kilometres, but for seven-year-old Toni—craning to watch his little town fold away behind the mountains as they trundled down the Rhine Valley toward Lake Constance—it was a move to another world. They reached their new home at night; streetcars were running along boulevards where elegantly dressed citizens were strolling past illuminated window-displays. He had never seen such opulence.

When Toni and his seven school-age siblings were enrolled at the local school (one child in virtually every grade), their homespun clothes and unfamiliarity with the German language initially earned them gibes as "gypsies from Graubünden." But they quickly established themselves as industrious students; in 1942, at the age of eleven, Cavelti followed his older brothers into the all-male Catholic high school attached to the local abbey, and it is possible to trace the earliest influences on Cavelti's artistry as a jeweller to his years there.

St. Gallen takes its name from the Benedictine abbey that was erected in the eighth century on the site of the cell of St. Gall, a sixth-century Irish missionary who—so legend has it—fell into a prickle bush, was helped out by a bear and, in gratitude, decided to stay in the high valley and preach Christianity to the local heathens. St. Gallen's fame as a centre of learning became widespread in the Middle Ages, and many illuminated manuscripts are preserved in the *Stiftsbibliotek*, the abbey library. Two or three times a year, the boys at the abbey school were encouraged to pull on felt overslippers (to protect the beautiful inlaid wooden floor against the scratches of their street shoes) and visit the library to inspect the showcases in which hundreds of handwritten books were displayed. Like the library floor, the books were pieces of art in themselves: both of the calligrapher's art and (in their elaborate hinges and closures) the goldsmith's art.

It was the beginning of an obsession that was to rule Cavelti's life. He filled school exercise books with calligraphy; he was fascinated, too, by the mechanics of the manuscripts—their bindings, the drawings they contained, the enamels with which they were decorated, the minute scale of their draughtsmanship. Never an outgoing child, he felt drawn to the slower, more focused lifestyle that had made such perfection possible, and discovered that he found much

The Cavelti children shortly before the family moved to St. Gallen. Toni is third from the left. All the clothes were handmade by their mother, Maria-Onna.

pleasure in the laborious creation of the beautiful and enduring object.

Soon it became clear that his direction was toward a
career involved in some way with the arts (he was hopeless at
arithmetic and algebra, though he excelled at geometry).
Amateur dramatics consumed much of his time. He would
organize plays and carnival dances for the Catholic youth
group attached to the abbey; for a youth who was so shy
that he would withdraw into uncommunicative muteness
whenever guests were invited to the family table, the chance
to dress up and assume another character became a means
of joyful escape.

At the age of fourteen, he joined St. Gallen's adult band
as a third-row clarinettist. He vaguely hoped to become a
professional musician, but soon realized that he didn't have
the talent, though he greatly values the four years he spent
with the Harmonie Musik—escorting the soccer team on its
triumphal parade from the railway station to the brewery, or
bringing the assembled townsfolk to their feet with a concert
performance of Khachaturian's *Sabre Dance*—because of
what the experience taught him about the difficulty of mas-
tering any art's complexities.

Music and the theatre were staples of his teenage years.
He would earn standing-room tickets at the opera house by
selling tickets for fund-raisers, and was able to see all the
popular operettas (Strauss, Lehár, Kalman) and a range of
operas and plays (though the school's principal, a clergyman,
would refuse to allow the free tickets to be used for plays
by, say, the humanist Goethe or for anything overtly anti-
Catholic). Opera remains a passion; he and his wife Hildegard
travel widely in North America to attend performances during
the season.

Industrious and ambitious, the teenage Cavelti spent much of his free time earning pocket money at various odd jobs—delivering newspapers, selling magazine subscriptions, working with the milk and bread roundsmen—and at the age of fifteen found a post as a handyman in a pastry shop. Always, though, the lure of the medieval craftsman's art hovered. Across the street from the pastry shop, as fate would have it, a goldsmith had his business. Cavelti would linger by the window and watch the care with which the craftsmen at their benches handled their small torches as they laboured to transform the drawings before them into three-dimensional objects. On warm days, the clear ring of their tiny hammers on the precious metals and the murmured advice of their overseer as he moved from bench to bench would float from the open casement, tantalizing him with visions of a career that was both aesthetically satisfying and (because he was a pragmatic Swiss) commercially profitable. He had no wish, after all, to spend his life being poor: what he wanted more than anything, even then, was to become a respected member of the community, a person of service, using his skills to make other people happy—a jeweller, why not?

So when, at the end of that school year, the pastry-shop proprietor offered him an apprenticeship, he shook his head and pointed across the street. "That's where I want to work," he said. The pastry-shop proprietor, perhaps recognizing the youth's abilities and sympathizing with his enthusiasms, walked across the street and conferred with the goldsmith. He returned with what was, for the eager young Cavelti, wonderful news. A new bench had just been installed; an apprentice was being sought. If Cavelti's parents were in agreement . . .

Young Toni started work as an apprentice to the goldsmith shortly before his sixteenth birthday. The following four years were, for him, years of glorious discovery. The gold-smith, Richard Bolli, proved to be far more than employer, far more than instructor—he was mentor, role model, articulator of principles that have guided Cavelti's work and thinking ever since. Bolli reinforced in the young man his enduring love of the well-made object: we are, he used to say, not merely makers of things, we are (he used the German word) *Kunsthandwerker*—literally, makers of art by hand, crafters of art.

Cavelti thrived. One day a week was spent with other apprentices at the town's trade school, bolstering the practical education provided by Bolli (gems, metals, tools, techniques) with courses in art history, design, accounting, creative writing, even public speaking—all of it designed to produce an individual properly equipped to make a smooth transition into a role as a valuable contributor to the well-oiled Swiss economy.

In the workshop, he was a natural. Within months of beginning his studies, he was creating jewellery. At the age of sixteen, he gave a cameo brooch surrounded by scrollwork to his mother. Bolli would tell the Cavelti parents about the keenness of their son's eye, the steadiness of his hand, his flair for the seamless zapping of a join—a little shot of flame, a neat solder just so, a bend, another zap of fire.

The examination at the end of the apprenticeship included a practical test. Candidates were briefly allowed to measure and sketch a ring, after which they were given eight hours to replicate it as closely as possible. Cavelti did so well his name was placed in the Golden Book of St. Gallen, a permanent celebration of civic achievers. He was nineteen.

To this day, Toni Cavelti, a man of self-effacing modesty, a man who has made jewellery for the Queen of England, resists the notion of the jeweller as an artist. Artists, he says, have the freedom to be bold, to use their imagination, to let

The young apprentice in Richard Bolli's *atelier* at St. Gallen, 1946.

AMETHYST - BROSCHE ANHÄNGER

Gelbgold 18 kt
Amethyst , 2 Brillanten

SEPTEMBER . 1949

BRILLANT - BROSCHE - ANHÄNGER

Gelbgold 18 kt
4 Brillanten
Fassungen Platin auf Weissgold

HERBST 1949

MÄSCHLIBROSCHE

Gelbgold 18 kt
4 Brillanten
Fassungen Platin auf Weissgold
3 x Ausgeführt   HERBST 1949

Pages of sketches from Toni
Cavelti's *Werkstatt Buch*.

their ideas roam free; he names, as examples, painters and sculptors who are his friends—his neighbour Gordon Smith, Jack Shadbolt, Toni Onley, Bill Reid. The jeweller, however, is a craftsman, at the service of his clients. Clients rarely want a piece of jewellery that reflects the maker's ideas—they want what's in their minds. Cavelti is prepared to admit that he harbours a secret hope that perhaps one day someone will choose not to wear an object he has made but, instead, put it under a glass dome and simply look at it: "the finest thing I could ever expect of my jewellery." At the same time, he knows that when a woman wears a piece of jewellery—and over 90 per cent of what Cavelti makes is for women—it has to be an expression of that woman.

"An artist is someone who works out of his head," he says, "disregarding public opinion or whether it sells. The moment you start listening to the client, you become a craftsman." The ultimate freedom of the creative artist is curtailed by someone else's tastes and needs. That's craft, says Cavelti, not art.

He applies that rule quite strictly. The illuminators of those medieval manuscripts at the St. Gallen abbey were, in his view, craftsmen. Michelangelo, when he was commissioned to paint the Sistine Chapel ceiling, was a craftsman. Fabergé, of fabulous jewellery fame? A craftsman too. Artists *per se* who have designed jewellery—Picasso, Giacometti— are a different matter. Few have been successful, and those who have—Dali, for instance, with his melting watches—have done none of the actual manufacture and have usually intended the pieces as freestanding works of art in themselves, rather than as items for functional adornment. For Cavelti, that doesn't count.

By no means everyone agrees with his own modest

assessment of his work. The painter Toni Onley, an early influence on Cavelti's design style, agrees that Cavelti is "linked to history" through his mastery of his craft, but argues that at that level, "Craft does spill over into artistry. In its highest sense, as embodied in someone like Toni Cavelti, jewellery becomes an art form." Sculptor Bill Reid, who shared a workshop with Cavelti for several years, agrees that it is precisely that mastery of the craft that allows art to emerge.

Inevitably, the years of apprenticeship developed in Cavelti a hunger for wider experience. He hoped first for Paris, but he needed a visa to be able to hold down a job there, and to get a visa he needed a job. Geneva, on Switzerland's southwestern border with France, was more fruitful ground; in 1951, at the age of twenty, shortly after completing his compulsory eighteen weeks of military training (in the Swiss heavy artillery), he left home to take up a new position at one of the dozens of *ateliers* that service the city's watch and jewellery trade. The move won only grudging approval from his parents; French-speaking Geneva at that time had a reputation as a lively, somewhat *louche* city, filled with nightclubs and pretty girls, and it was made clear to the young bachelor, on his first foray away from the family home, that he must look out for himself and be a good boy.

Fulfilling his military service obligation, the young soldier mans the controls of a Swiss artillery cannon.

Life in Geneva was a far cry from life in St. Gallen—and not merely (or even) because of the nightclubs and the girls. It became evident very quickly that he could set aside his cherished notions of *Kunsthandwerk*. His job at the *atelier*, in a big, gloomy industrial building on the banks of the Rhône river, was more like being part of a commercial production line. Speed was of the essence. An order would come in from a watch or jewellery designer, sometimes in the half-million-dollar price range, and the task of creating the multiple elements of the design would be distributed to the workers along the bench with no concern (or time) for individual pride in the finished object.

Cavelti, a young newcomer, was initially given the lowliest tasks, making what jewellers call "findings"—safety catches, joints, platinum tubing. He found the work dispiriting, the conditions discouraging, the atmosphere depressing. The jobbing work, turning out stock for jewellery stores according to the season's fashions, was a far cry from what he believed he had been trained for. With the freshness and eagerness of youth, he had expected to be able to use his skills and artistry to contribute in a positive and creative way to the development of his chosen craft; instead, he found himself stifled and frustrated by the heavy hand of tradition.

His human contacts were no better. While the *atelier* owner made it clear that he had hired Cavelti because he had a great admiration for *les Grisonais*, the people of Graubünden, the shop foreman seemed to take an instant dislike to the young newcomer. Co-workers were always being fired; it was hard to make friends. And on the one occasion when he did manage to meet someone of like mind, a co-worker named Gilbert Albert who liked to talk of the craft of jewellery in the same idealistic manner as Cavelti, the man was dismissed within months of his arrival, barely giving the two a chance to begin to become friends. The firing did little to damage Albert's career. He went on to become design head of the renowned watch house Patek Philippe, and today is considered one of the leading designers of jewellery in Europe, in such demand that he is one of the very few modern jewellers—and Cavelti smiles when he mentions this—who can afford to be an artist as well as a craftsman.

Cavelti's other co-workers at the *atelier* were a motley crew: an elderly French communist who resented having to work for the Swiss rich, but who introduced Cavelti to the pleasures of sitting in sidewalk cafés sipping a *Suze à l'eau* and watching the girls go by; a family man who had spent time on an Israeli kibbutz and consistently complained that he couldn't make ends meet on the meagre salary offered at the *atelier*. It was not what Cavelti had imagined, and he became progressively disenchanted with his life. Uncomfortable in what he felt was an unwelcoming city, he took to spending hours alone, wandering Geneva's old town, wondering why he bothered with jewellery any more, knowing he couldn't go on doing what he was doing for the rest of his days, pondering his future.

One day, someone handed his future to him.

It was a Sunday afternoon. He was walking by the river, and spotted a poster pinned to a utility pole advertising an exhibition at the Hôtel du Rhône—a free display of paintings called *Cities of Canada*. He had nothing more pressing to do; he went. He was entranced. The scenes, all by Canadian artists, showed cities from Victoria, B.C., to St. John's, Newfoundland. But the one that caught his eye was a painting of the downtown Vancouver skyline seen from the water, the art deco Marine Building on the waterfront, tugs busy below it.

As he left, he exchanged the French-language catalogue he had been given when he entered the show for an English version. It was a symbolic gesture; he had reached a time for the burning of bridges, and had made up his mind that he was going to give up his career in jewellery, leave Switzerland and make a new life in Canada. In English Canada: Vancouver. He spoke no English, and had only the haziest notions of Canada: a country of mountains, ice, snow, cold winters…a bigger, less civilized Switzerland. He planned to find work as a lumberjack.

This was 1954; in those days the formalities for entry to Canada were simple. Two days after visiting the art show, he travelled to Lausanne, where the Canadian Pacific office functioned as an agency for Canadian immigration. He was X-rayed, examined by a doctor and declared to be precisely the kind of healthy, robust young individual Canada wished to welcome. Where would he like to go? He named Vancouver. The immigration officer shook his head: a person who spoke no English should go to Montreal. Cavelti demurred: Vancouver was his goal. Very well, said the immigration officer. We'll indicate Montreal as your intended destination, but as soon as you get there you'll have the right as a new Canadian to go where you like. Well, thought Cavelti, how generous: a genuinely free country.

The Swiss have been an *émigré* nation since long before the first contingent of the Swiss guard decamped for Rome in 1505 to protect the Pope, so his parents took the news with good grace: just so long, they said, as he promised to come home in two years and not stay in North America for decades, like his three uncles. He promised.

It all happened in a rush: Basel…Paris…Le Havre and the ageing Cunard steamer *Scythia*, then a lurching, seasick plunge through high spring seas across the Atlantic to Quebec City. At the urging of one of his brothers, he carried along his jeweller's tools. He could always sell them for cash if he fell on hard times.

The trip seemed blessed by good omens. On the ship, which carried mainly immigrants, he met several individuals who had been prisoners of war in Canada and had been so

Toni Cavelti en route to a new life in Canada on board the *Scythia*, June 1954.

impressed by the friendliness and decency of their Canadian captors that they were returning to find a new life there. And in Montreal he and another young Swiss who had accompanied him from Geneva met another immigrant, a German, who found them a place to stay and smoothed their first days in the new country.

Montreal, though, was not Cavelti's destination. Soon, he and his Swiss companion were on board the trans-Canada train, living off the dark bread, cheese and sausage they had bought in Montreal to sustain them until they reached the distant city that they planned to make their home. As, mile by mile, the future drew nearer, they became more nervous; Cavelti eyed the toolbox he had so fortuitously been persuaded to carry and wondered whether the lumber industry was, after all, quite such a good idea.

Still, they were young, they were on the biggest adventure of their lives, and on their last night on the train, as it steamed and thundered toward the British Columbia sunset, they sat down at a linen-covered table in the luxury of the dining room and shared a last good meal before their new lives began.

Toni Cavelti stepped off the train in Vancouver on the early morning of his twenty-third birthday, June 13, 1954. He was wearing a new suit he had had made for the occasion—Prince of Wales pattern—and a smart tie. He had landed-immigrant papers, a box of jeweller's tools and exactly eight dollars to his name. He did not speak English. He was in for some serious culture shock.

On the platform to meet him was Max Bissegger, a friend from St. Gallen who had emigrated to Canada a year before. Cavelti had seen the photos of his friend's success in the New

World on the walls of Bissegger's parents' home, posing with his green U.S. station wagon, the hood raised to show the wondering Swiss the enormous engine. The very vehicle was there at the Vancouver station to meet him, and Cavelti expressed polite admiration for the way Bissegger had been able to establish himself in his new country so quickly. Bissegger kicked the car's tires. "This damn thing isn't paid for," he said. "Nobody pays for anything here. It's all borrowed money." It was Cavelti's introduction to the North American credit system. He would get to know it well.

Bissegger drove Cavelti around the city, showing him the sights. And as they stood by the *Empress of Japan* figurehead in Stanley Park and looked at the mountains, the graceful Lions Gate Bridge arching across the narrows, Bissegger's sad story came out. Despite the brave face he had put on for his family, he had no prospects, he was unemployed (he was by profession a floorlayer), he was living on loans, he was going to have to go home.

But meanwhile, he said, he hoped Toni would fare better. He had found a contact in the jewellery business, a representative of a German maker of imitation jewellery, who was willing to ask around on Toni's behalf. It would be necessary, though, for Cavelti to do two things if he ever hoped to find a job—learn English, and buy some blue jeans to replace that terrible suit.

Cavelti felt affronted. He had never worn jeans in his life, and he hadn't come to Canada to wear common working clothes. He swore then that he never would wear jeans, and—despite their universal fashion in later years—he never has.

Bissegger's despondency over his own future was short-lived. A week after Cavelti's arrival, he met a young woman at a dance—he and Cavelti were there together—and fell wildly in love. A year later, Cavelti was the best man at their wedding. Soon, Bissegger established a successful floorlaying company of his own, acquired a substantial tract of land in the fast-developing southwest corner of British Columbia, and never looked back.

Cavelti was not going to escape the clutches of his fate as easily as he had planned. He had been persuaded to bring his jeweller's tools for a reason. Bissegger's German friend, Peter Gaupp, had wide contacts in the jewellery trade. Their first stop was Vancouver's principal jewellery store, Birks, at the central intersection of Georgia and Granville Streets. The manager minced no words: he had no need for jewellers, since the company did the bulk of its manufacturing in eastern Canada. Cavelti should have stayed there.

At O.B. Allan, then an important jewellery retailer, he was told he was overqualified; his designs were too sophisticated. At Trayling and Waters, jewellery wholesalers, he was again turned down. The company, which had at one time employed about two dozen jewellers on its benches, had just come through a devastating strike in which it, too, had discovered that it was cheaper to manufacture in eastern Canada.

Despairing, Cavelti went walking on his own. On his travels with Gaupp around the city core, he had spotted a jewellery store under the name of Firbanks. He retraced his steps and, in halting English, offered his drawings to the man behind the counter. There was, once more, no job; but this time he was referred to the workshop that produced all the trade commissions for the store. Maybe employment might be found there?

The workshop proprietor was a Czech *émigré* named Frank E. Bercha. (Like Cavelti, he was born with only one given name: the middle E was an invention he added himself, he told Cavelti later, because "in this country you cannot get by with only one name." The E stood for Emily, his wife.) Bercha greeted Cavelti with hands smeared with polishing rouge. Cavelti took to him immediately. He was the first jeweller he had met in this far-flung outpost who seemed to actually do his own work.

Bercha wasn't so impressed. He told Cavelti frankly he was out of his mind. To leave *Switzerland* for *Canada*? He himself was a refugee from Prague; he had had to flee to Bogotá, where everything was crooked; moreover he had been extremely sick (and here he opened up his shirt to show his scar), such food, such people, and now, here, Vancouver. What a fool you are, Cavelti, to leave *Switzerland*, where I and my family were once refugees, given shelter above a stable in the Emmental, the happiest weeks of our lives, I would *pay* to get those times back, and you are *leaving*? Abruptly, Bercha brought out drawings of some sophisticated platinum drop earrings. There was a chance he would get the order for them, he said; if he did, could Cavelti make them? No problem, said Cavelti: I've got my tools right here at my lodgings. Bercha took his address and said he'd get in touch if the order came through.

It did, he did, and by mid-morning the next day Cavelti was at work. Conditions were by no means wonderful. The materials that were provided were mismatched and shoddy, there was no emery paper to provide the necessary finish (when Bercha agreed to go across the street to the Hudson's Bay Company to buy supplies, he came back with sandpaper, not the emery paper needed for filing a tough metal like platinum) and the work wasn't really much different from what Cavelti had left Geneva to escape. But Cavelti, swallowing hard, turned out a very satisfactory pair of earrings in rapid time and suddenly found himself employed.

The rate was a dollar an hour—good money, by Swiss standards: it allowed Cavelti to maintain a reasonable room in an old house in the city's West End, eat at the European cafés that lined Robson Street, and even pay for evening classes in spoken English. And when Cavelti (learning quickly) told Bercha within a matter of months that he was planning to go to work in a sawmill to improve his income, the money became even better.

Bercha and his wife saw themselves as displaced members of the Czech aristocracy, forced against their will to assume refugee status in Canada, all the glamour of their Prague salon reduced to photos on their West Vancouver living-room walls. An air of muted tragedy hung about them—not just because of their circumstances, but because of the loss of Bercha's beloved brother, himself a famed jeweller in Prague: he had been due to leave with them, but had died days before departure.

Cavelti provided a connection, however tenuous, with the Old Country. He was a frequent guest at their home. On weekends, he and Bercha would go angling for groundfish in a rented boat from Horseshoe Bay. Later, when Cavelti bought his first car (it cost him $700), Bercha would invite him over for a Sunday-morning car wash (Bercha had no car of his own) and they would go for a drive.

Once, soon after Cavelti's arrival in Vancouver, Bercha gave him a ticket for a sporting event at the newly built Empire Stadium. Cavelti, no follower of the sports pages, had no idea what to expect, but, not wanting to seem ungracious, put on his best suit and tie and walked across the city to the stadium. He witnessed one of the most dramatic events in the history of sport: Roger Bannister's defeat of John Landy in the famous "miracle mile."

Through Bercha, Cavelti made his first contacts with the group of influential Czech immigrant entrepreneurs who did so much to develop the B.C. forest industry in the middle part of the century—the Koerners, the Prentices, the Bentleys: customers of Bercha and, much later, customers of Cavelti.

He was under no illusions about the jobbing work Bercha undertook for the city's jewellery stores. It was Geneva all over again, writ small. But conditions were better, the city was more amenable, people were friendlier, and he genuinely liked his employer. He became the firm's mainstay, someone who could always be relied on to deliver high-quality work in a hurry. A ring order had been forgotten and was needed by noon? Toni would save the day, rooting through the old-gold box for cut-up oddments (a shank, a head) that he could do something with. Mr. Pastinsky needed some more cufflinks with Hebrew letters superimposed on textured gold? Over to Toni; Bercha would do the polishing. "Toni," Bercha once told him after he'd saved the day once again, "you are even better than my brother." It was the ultimate compliment.

One of the retailers from whom Bercha took assignments was a flamboyant young German immigrant named Karl Stittgen. At the time, he operated a store in West Vancouver, primarily selling watches but increasingly moving into the area of jewellery: he would buy small antique brooches and run them over to Bercha in his patched-up silver MG to have them turned into rings. Big, showy rings.

He and Cavelti, about the same age, speaking the same language, became friends. Evenings, they'd go to a movie, then cruise over to the White Spot drive-in, eating hamburgers from a narrow tray across the front seats of the sportscar. Weekends, they'd motor up the Fraser Valley to Cultus Lake with Stittgen's lively German-Austrian crowd. It seemed natural for them to go into business together.

So about eighteen months after arriving in Canada, Cavelti said his farewells to the Berchas and set up his own shop, on a rent-sharing basis, in Stittgen's Marine Drive store in West Vancouver's Ambleside district: *European Watchmakers and Jewellers*, said the new illuminated sign.

Determined to do it properly, Cavelti invested $1,800 in the enterprise. It was all the money he had saved since his arrival in Canada. He built a workbench, a showcase, bought more tools, installed equipment (rolling mills, draw plates to extrude gold wire to various thicknesses) and, when everything was ready, sent off an order to a Toronto gold-supply company for a sheet of 18-carat gold. The order came to $280; when it arrived, Cavelti had to rush next door to the grocer to cash a cheque so he could pay the postman who brought the little parcel. He had meanwhile bought a handful of semiprecious stones; he fashioned the gold and the stones into modest rings and put them on display in the store window. One sold almost immediately—a $110 cash sale. He was on his way.

If location is everything in retailing, this particular location certainly paid off for Cavelti—not in terms of financial success (business was not particularly brisk) but in terms of connections and new influences.

Above the premises he shared with Stittgen was the New Design Gallery, owned by Abraham Rogatnick and Alvin Balkind. Rogatnick taught architecture at the University of British Columbia; Balkind was a writer, critic and later curator of the UBC Fine Arts Gallery. They had moved to Vancouver

An early advertisement for the Cavelti-Stittgen enterprise in the *West Vancouver News*, 1957.

from the U.S. and opened the New Design Gallery in December 1955. Widely credited in later years with bringing in an infusion of ideas and energy that helped transform the face of art-making in Vancouver, they made modernism their focus. Most of the city's prominent and rising artists of the day—Jack Shadbolt, Gordon Smith, Takao Tanabe, Don Jarvis, Bruno and Molly Bobak—exhibited regularly at their gallery.

For Cavelti, it was an eye-opener. He would spend hours sitting on the back steps behind the building talking with Balkind, and quickly got to know the artists, architects and art enthusiasts who thronged the upstairs gallery. More important than the personal contacts, though, were the creative influences. The example of his new artist friends encouraged him to experiment with unusual designs, often influenced by the art that was going on around him. And it is possible to see, in his work from that period, echoes of the lyrical, organic forms that were appearing on the canvases of Vancouver's modernist painters of the time: Toni Onley, whose abstractions in the late 1950s and early 1960s sent the whole town in new directions; Jack Shadbolt, with his ecstatic delight in colour and abstract form; Gordon Smith's cool landscapes, as well as the organic forms and juxtaposed shapes and angles of Arthur Erickson's architecture.

In a catalogue entry for a 1967 show at the UBC Fine Arts Gallery, Balkind caught precisely the condition of art-making in Vancouver in that period: "In this remote, un-crowded, lotus-eating city, seemingly far from many of the world's agonies and excesses, there is room for art to grow, even in the face of (or perhaps because of) vast public and official indifference." He spoke, in particular, about the "buoyancy, optimism, love of materials, delight in colour and form, and lightness of spirit" that Vancouver artists expressed in their

Gordon Smith
Red Painting, 1957
Vancouver Art Gallery 57.5

Toni Onley
Collage #7, 1958
Vancouver Art Gallery 58.8

work. Toni Cavelti, recognizing that one certain way to improve on the quality of jewellery-making in the city (and thus improve his own sales opportunities) was to introduce new styles and designs, began to translate that spirit into his creations. He became the jeweller-bearer of the banner of '60s art in the city.

One of his most enduring friendships from those years is with Bill Reid. Reid was drawn by Cavelti's skills—one of the first things Cavelti taught him was the tricky task of making clasps that would click and hinges that would allow a necklace to sit properly on the wearer—and developed the habit of stopping in at Cavelti's workshop with small commissions, or to show him his latest creations. Soon, Reid had "adopted" the young jeweller, and began to introduce him to his customers; these, too, subsequently became regulars of Cavelti himself. Reid also arranged for Cavelti to get a job teaching jewellery-making at the University of British Columbia extension department, but that didn't last long: Cavelti resigned after one term, disgusted by the attitudes of his "students," most of them elderly individuals more interested in the profits they could make than in the making of jewellery.

For Cavelti himself, however, belief in his calling still burned bright. In 1957 he spotted an advertisement in a jewellery trade magazine inviting entries for a competition sponsored by the De Beers corporation. The Diamonds International Award was the Oscar of the jewellery industry; several famous names had won it in previous years (among them, Cavelti's former colleague from Geneva, Gilbert Albert).

Cavelti, released from any constraints about materials by his belief that he didn't have a chance of winning, spent a Sunday afternoon sketching a ring featuring five large baguette-cut diamonds set so that, viewed from above, they gave the impression of five high-rise buildings in a cityscape. He copied the design onto a piece of card, sent it to New York, and thought no more about it. Two weeks later, a telegram arrived telling him he had won the prize.

Cavelti duly made up the design and put it in the store window, priced at $900. One afternoon a man came in and said he would buy it—but when Cavelti examined the cheque the man offered, it was only made out for $500.

"I'm sorry," said Cavelti, "but the price is $900."

The ring that won the 1957 Diamonds International Award.

"That's what you think," said the customer. "I think it's only worth $500."

"Sir," said the ever-polite Cavelti. "No—$900."

"Who do you think you are?" said the customer. "I'm offering you $500—it's a very good price for this ring."

But Cavelti remained adamant, and finally the customer stormed out without the ring. The next night, the store was burgled and the ring was stolen—"So $500," he says ruefully, "would have been a very good price."

The publicity Toni Cavelti received for the Diamonds International Award (and for the ring's theft) persuaded him it was time to move on. He had had a wonderful time in West Vancouver, but he was convinced he had to get out from beneath the shadow of the (as he believed) smarter, better-looking, better-spoken Stittgen if he was to make anything of himself.

It was more of a struggle than he had anticipated. To offset the costs of setting up a new business alone, he entered into a brief partnership with Robert Droz, a young Swiss watchmaker he met at a party. They set up a small store in the narrow hallway arcade of the Burrard Building, located downtown at the central Georgia and Burrard Streets intersection; the cheerful Stittgen helped them build the display cases.

Despite Cavelti's growing public profile, business was terrible. Some months after opening, Cavelti had a nightmare about a break-in during which all their inventory was stolen. The following weekend a break-in actually occurred; after using the insurance payout to settle with customers and suppliers, he and Droz found themselves penniless. Ironically, however, the publicity generated by the robbery attracted new customers, some with quite substantial commissions, and Cavelti decided to look for a spot where he could establish a business of his own.

Location, again, played a crucial part in his future. Reasoning that a successful business's good fortune rubs off on its neighbours, he set out to place himself as close as possible to the city's most successful jeweller, Birks.

Slyly claiming that jewellery repairs were his business's principal concern, he persuaded an agent to lease him a space on the second floor of the Birks building, directly above the store. There he set about building a serious *clientèle*, using selective advertising in newspapers, magazines and theatre programs, and mailing personal letters inviting business and commissions to prominent local citizens whose names he found in the newspaper. Everywhere, he used the Birks address to maximum advantage.

In the summer of 1959, five years after his arrival in Canada, he made good, belatedly, on his parting promise to his parents, and made his first return visit to Switzerland. Three weeks later he returned to Canada engaged to be married.

He had known Hildegard Moser since they were children in St. Gallen; they had met from time to time in Geneva, where she occasionally travelled on business as directrice of a fashion salon, and while they were never formally attached as a couple, a fondness certainly existed. He carried a photo of her in his wallet throughout his early years in Canada, and when he arrived in Switzerland he enlisted the help of one of his sisters, a friend of Hildegard, to re-establish contact.

They met the next day, and the next. He had to go to Basel to a jewellery fair, she had to go to Basel on fashion business; they went to Basel together and spent the day at

Hildegard Cavelti in the 1950s.

the zoo. A week after he arrived back in Switzerland, he asked her to marry him. She agreed, but it couldn't be immediate. Her contract with her fashion house required her to finish the collection on which she was working.

Cavelti returned to Canada and set about preparing for the wedding. In Squamish, he found a priest who could conduct the service in Swiss-German. He booked a place for a reception. He bought some cases of Riesling. He sent out invitations to eighty of his friends. In Switzerland meanwhile, Hildegard, an accomplished seamstress, fashioned her wedding dress and assembled her trousseau.

Hildegard arrived in Vancouver on a Friday in October 1959. The following day they attended Bill Reid's wedding. Hildegard remembers the way fellow-guests Abraham Rogatnick and Alvin Balkind talked to her in French, going out of their way to make her feel welcome. "My English wasn't good: I had lived many years in the French part of Switzerland and I thought Canada was bilingual so I'd have no problem because everyone would speak French."

A week later, Toni and Hildegard celebrated their own marriage at St. Anthony's Roman Catholic Church in West Vancouver. The ring that he slipped onto her finger during the ceremony was a gold and diamond band in an open, abstract design that he had made according to sizings Hildegard had airmailed to him. His own broad gold ring had been fashioned in a snatched hour at the bench the night before.

Hildegard's re-entry into his life marked the beginning of a rise to a new level of success for Cavelti. There was still not much money in the business, and most of what did come in was immediately reinvested in gems, gold and platinum, but they both knew how to make ends meet. Happy and exhilarated, he began to become more daring in his designs. And now, earlier contacts began to pay off.

One of the most fruitful was with a Vancouver socialite he had first encountered at his tiny store in the Burrard Building in 1957. At the time, she had been the secretary to one of the most powerful businessmen in Vancouver; she was fascinated by his creations, and he made a number of modest things for her. "One of these days," she told him, "I may be a very good customer for you." She was as good as her word; not long after she and Cavelti first met, she married her employer, and soon Cavelti was making rings and other items on a regular basis for the couple. It became more than a business relationship. He and Hildegard were frequent guests at the couple's home, and he credits the woman with introducing him and his work to many of her well-to-do friends, who in turn became his customers.

His reputation continued to grow. In 1961 he was the only Canadian jeweller invited to participate in an exhibition of contemporary jewellery at Goldsmith Hall in London, England. He sent a piece that echoed his past and spoke about his present—a perfectly prismatic uncut white quartz crystal from Grisons, the Swiss canton where he was born, set in a modernistic gold frame embellished with platinum and diamonds.

Business was also stimulated by the presence of Bill Reid, who for a time moved his bench into Cavelti's shop and brought in a steady stream of customers attracted by fine design. Soon, the Birks building manager began to drop hints that no one would mind if Cavelti were to break his lease and move away—as far away as possible. At the time, Cavelti had no intention of doing so. In 1963, however, his plans took a sudden shift. That February, he and Hildegard took a cheap charter flight to Switzerland to show their one-year-old son,

A piece of rock crystal from the Swiss Alps, set in a structure of round gold wire with platinum triangles *pavé*-set with 80 diamonds, displayed at Goldsmith Hall in London, England, 1961.

Chris, to their families. He was the first Cavelti born in Canada; everyone demanded a visit.

To get a break from the incessant housecalls, Toni and Hildegard left the baby with one of his sisters in St. Gallen and took the train to Geneva, the city he had left in search of a new life in Canada, to renew acquaintance with his old boss at the *atelier*. They were welcomed and fêted like returning royalty; and as they sat in the dining car of the train taking them back to St. Gallen, sipping Swiss white wine and watching the neat, orderly towns and manicured countryside flash by, they realized afresh just how beautiful Switzerland was and how much they missed it. They resolved right there, on the train, to close down the business in Canada, sell their few possessions and return to their homeland to start a new life.

High on hope and dreams, he advertised in a newspaper for work, was invited to become a salesman with a jewellery company in Lucerne and agreed to do everything he could to make the move before the start of the summer tourist season. Filled with thoughts of their new-shaped future, the couple returned to Vancouver, determined to wind up their affairs as fast as possible. Friends put in bids for the Rosenthal china, the crystal, the cutlery, the napery that had come to Canada as part of Hildegard's trousseau.

But by then it was spring. Vancouver was at its most seductive—the trees in blossom, the air sweet with flowers and the sea, the evenings fresh and easy. Slowly, the idyll of a West Coast springtime worked its magic; slowly, the idea of going back to Europe lost its charm. A salesman—how could he have agreed to such a job? And what about their baby, Chris? Surely it was only fair that a child born a Canadian citizen should have the opportunity to grow up in his native country.

What clinched it was an offer from a watch-company

salesman for their entire possessions. Suddenly, the realization of the enormity of what they were contemplating hit them. And after a sleepless night, Vancouver became their embraced home. This, they realized, was where their lives were; this was where their future would unfold.

If attitude shapes destiny, this was the moment that marked the beginning of Cavelti's most productive and creative years—and his most exciting as a businessman. In his new mood of optimism and confidence, realizing that his little upstairs shop, with its average gross of around $1,600 a month, offered only limited chances of growth, he began to search for a more substantial and visible retail outlet. However, one principle of business never left him: he always believed proximity to the city's prime jewellery retailer to be of crucial importance, so he was jubilant when he discovered a space at the other end of the block from Birks at 717 Seymour Street.

It was part of the frontage of the old Strand Theatre, in its day a handsome brick structure fronting West Georgia Street, but by that time shabby and dilapidated. It didn't even have a street entrance, but Cavelti, filled with can-do optimism, was not to be deterred. On a limited budget, Victoria architect Peter Cotton designed a little jewel of a store—three small show windows on Seymour Street, a stained-glass entrance door, elegant steps up to the showroom, a bench at the back behind a glass door so customers could see the master at work—and they were on their way.

These were years when everything seemed to come together in an ideal synthesis. As the store attracted more and more clients, his reputation became more and more firmly established, much of it by the private, word-of-mouth recommendation that is the cornerstone of success in a business like Cavelti's. A valuable contact of this kind was the owner of one of Vancouver's last *haute couture* houses. Lore Maria Weiner operated a fashionable workshop making costumes for ladies of society. She took a liking to Cavelti and his creations and would frequently send her clients to his store for a custom necklace or a pair of earrings to complete the ensemble she had created.

In turn, that growing acceptance by his *clientèle* gave him the confidence to strike out in new directions. Training, inclination and opportunity fostered the production of a host of daring new designs. The contemporary trends in art and architecture that had influenced him since his first contacts with the New Design Gallery played an increasingly large role in his work. He would go to the galleries to see what Toni Onley or Jack Shadbolt was up to, or he'd drive around the city to see Arthur Erickson's latest concrete structure, then return to his bench and see how those ideas might translate into jewellery, using the raw materials of his own trade.

A specialist since his apprentice days in the structural aspects of goldsmithing, he experimented with new ways to manipulate fine gold and platinum wire to make structures whose delicate and fragile appearance belied their sturdy strength. His early, painstaking mastery of technique made the quality of his work impossible to match by cruder mass-manufacturing methods; everything he did was one-of-a-kind, uniquely styled by a master craftsman to suit the tastes of the purchaser. Customers began to commission him to make whole suites of jewellery, sight unseen, trusting in his judgement, discretion and sensitivity.

In this period he won two more Diamonds International Awards, both for pieces that exemplified the mix of exuberance and good taste that characterized his flights of design

The influence of the architectural style of Arthur Erickson (designer of Simon Fraser University, shown in the photograph below) is clearly evident in these three rings by Cavelti. In addition, the chunky, unpolished gold castings on highly polished shanks echo Erickson's characteristic use of raw concrete.

The brooch-pendant that won the Diamonds International Award for 1963 features a baroque South Seas pearl surrounded by yellow diamonds, *pavé*-set white diamonds and free-floating marquis-cut diamonds.

The winner of a special best-of-show award at the 1963 Diamonds International Awards: a delicate, airy brooch in the unmistakable Cavelti style of the period.

imagination in those years. One was for a platinum brooch-pendant that featured a South Seas pearl surrounded by golden diamonds and a splash effect created by hundreds of tiny, full-cut diamonds. The other—voted by the jury as the most exciting piece of all the Diamonds International Award winners that year—was for a spidery wire brooch in gold and diamonds. He was on top of his world.

One of the appeals of Toni Cavelti's designs is the way they so artfully bridge the millennia. Often, his use of gold and gems has a prehistoric, mythic dimension—a raw brutalism of texture that hints at the trade's relationship to the earth, to the arching history of civilizations. And he admires the work of the ancients quite sincerely. When he visited the exhibition of the fabled gold of Tutankhamen some years ago, he was in awe of the quality of the *repoussé* work: "I couldn't come close—it was done 3,000 years ago, but it's artistry that we can't even comprehend." Yet he never lets himself fall back into the hackneyed ways of the past; rather, he is forever searching out new approaches to design that express the imaginative vigour of the times in which he lives.

That vigour, though, must sometimes be tempered by practicality. Jewellery-making is perhaps the most stressful of all the manufacturing arts because it holds so much potential for financial loss. A misplaced cut as a lapidary trims off flaws and inclusions can decimate a stone's value; a careless tap of a hammer as a gold clasp is beaten into place can break a $25,000 emerald—Cavelti has seen it happen. The softer stones, like aquamarine and tourmaline, are easy to nick. Inevitably, stress takes its toll. Cavelti has seen many jobbing gemstone setters become alcoholics in their forties, and few setters are able to work beyond the age of sixty.

And the physical demands increase as the body ages. Now in his mid-sixties, he thinks it is time to wind down his involvement in the manufacture of his designs. That's one of the reasons he's happy to employ a team of craftsmen in his upstairs workshop—they're skilled at handling the physical detail that no longer comes easily to him, allowing him to spend more time on the refinement of the design.

What remains, though, is the artistic visionary. Cavelti is one of those rare individuals (others exist in the antiques trade, or in the business of clocks and watches) who recognize quality and potential instantly, instinctively, without conscious effort, in a prickling of the scalp or a quickening of the blood. He can take a dealer's proffered package of gems and in a matter of moments the stones that interest him will catch his eye—and (integral to the process of discovery) he will immediately begin to envision the object he will fashion around them.

A flamboyant two-finger ring, a popular item in the booming Vancouver of the early 1970s.

In 1972 his elder brother Franz, who had emigrated to Canada in 1958, moved to Vancouver from Whitehorse, where he had been working in the communications industry. His training in Switzerland had been as a *Schlosser*—a cross between a mechanic and a blacksmith in the metalworking trade. Franz joined the Cavelti business and became a valuable member of the shop team, where he still specializes in model-making and foundry work. Cavelti claims Franz is a better designer than he is, and, as evidence, points to his brother's sun design, which has become one of the workshop's most popular limited edition pieces, his series of zodiac signs, the multitude of charms he has created, and the Giacometti-style sculpture of a couple that Cavelti commissioned from Franz to decorate the store's entranceway.

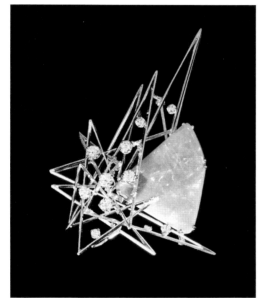

For Cavelti, the 1960s and 1970s were a period of creative experiment and imaginative discovery. These three exuberant designs are typical of that time: (*left*) a brooch highlighting a freeform opal set in a dazzle of diamond-set, knife-edge gold wire; (*centre*) a brooch featuring polished gold squares dancing across an irregular-shaped, rough-textured gold sheet dusted with pure gold grain; (*right*) a brooch-pendant expressing classic modernity in its intriguingly asymmetrical disk of satiny gold and a contrasting angular shape textured with gold grain.

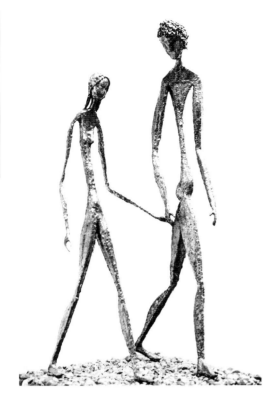

A welded metal sculpture by Franz Cavelti on display at the Seymour Street salon.

With his brother minding the store, Cavelti was able to take his wife and (by now) two children on a European motoring tour. When they returned home, he found the Strand Theatre building in which the store was housed was to be demolished. Once again, he was walking the streets and talking to agents, looking for a new home not far from the powerful Birks magnet.

He found the ideal spot in the middle of the 600 block on Seymour Street—less than a block north of the previous store, and just around the corner from Birks. The owners, two elderly Seattle women, agreed to sell it to him for $100,000, on a small downpayment and a twenty-year mortgage. For Cavelti, this move from rental to ownership marked real security at last. He hired his friend Zoltan Kiss, the architect who was to create the Caveltis' West Vancouver home, to design the new premises.

However, before he could move in, he was approached by a real estate agent offering to buy the property and proposing to double his downpayment. Cavelti refused; he had no wish or intention to sell. But the agent steadily increased his offer until Cavelti felt it was impossible to continue to turn the man down. In any case, he had used the intervening period to scout out yet another property, just a few steps south at 692 Seymour. He pocketed the profit from the sale and used it to install and equip a handsome new store at the new location, with benches for six jewellers behind the showroom.

In terms of prosperity, these were some of Vancouver's best years. Real estate was booming, the city was flourishing, the resource industries that provide the financial backbone for the British Columbia economy were thriving. Cavelti's customers—some of them instant millionaires from the stock market or real estate development—began to demand bigger and more intricate work. People would drop in to buy $50,000 rings without batting an eyelid. At one point, Cavelti had ten jewellers on his benches, helping to service an international *clientèle*.

Steadily, just as he had dreamed when he stood outside the jeweller's window in St. Gallen, Cavelti had built for himself a position of trust and respect in the community. He was doing what gave him the greatest satisfaction—using his hard-won skills to make a good living at the service of others. Though not always: in 1971 he was commissioned by the British Columbia government to make a necklace of B.C. gold nuggets and local jade (nephrite) for the Queen, to mark a royal visit to the province on the centenary of British Columbia's entry into the Confederation of Canada. Because of the potential for embarrassment at the notion of extravagant government spending, the commission was funnelled through the Department of Highways, and a suggestion from Cavelti that it include one hundred diamonds to commemorate the centenary was rejected as too expensive. The province eventually paid, via the Highways department, a sum that barely covered Cavelti's costs.

However, his most expensive mistake in those halcyon years was his decision to expand the business and open a second store at the Oakridge shopping centre, in a well-to-do residential area of south Vancouver. No expense was spared. Precast concrete, solid marble, fine carpeting and first-class woodwork made it one of the most handsome stores of any kind in the city. But he had overlooked a crucial element of the mix. At the heart of the Toni Cavelti mystique, the reason why his *clientèle* stuck by him so loyally, was Toni Cavelti himself. Every individual who walked through the doors of his salons expected to be waited on by the master. Without his

Her Majesty Queen Elizabeth II at a state dinner in Victoria in 1971, wearing, much to Cavelti's delight, the necklace commissioned from him by the B.C. government and presented to her earlier that day.

presence, it was just another jewellery retail outlet. So while prospects at Oakridge at first seemed auspicious, sales soon became stagnant and then began to sink. After seven years (as early as the lease allowed), he pulled out. He had learned a valuable lesson.

In the mid-1970s, Cavelti bought a half interest in the Randall Building, an old and run-down commercial structure at 555 West Georgia Street, a block and a half east of Birks. Here he established a design studio and workshop, where he and his craftsmen colleagues created many of the superb pieces that were sold at the Seymour Street premises just around the corner. However, in the late 1980s he and his partners in the enterprise were approached by Grosvenor International, the Duke of Westminster's property company, with a request to sell. The building was part of a larger parcel the company wanted to buy; there were plans for a new high-rise. The only missing part of the jigsaw was the Randall Building.

The partners were eager to accept the offer. Cavelti said no. The developers steadily pushed the price higher. Cavelti remained adamant. His twenty-year lease on Seymour Street was almost up; the Randall Building was the perfect spot for a new home for his store. Threats of court action ensued; finally, Cavelti himself bought out his partners—at a by then hugely inflated price—and sent the developers packing.

Always a touch uncomfortable with the idea of free time, never an aficionado of games and diversions, Toni Cavelti prefers to find a creative outlet for his energies. The Randall Building arrived at precisely the right time: he was approaching the age of sixty, and while he still enjoyed the craft of making jewellery—he even fancied he was getting better at it— he was itching for a new creative challenge.

The process of acquiring the building and turning it into the kind of headquarters he had always envisioned for his business gave him new vigour, and he threw himself into the task with conviction and passion, determined to create a jewel of a setting in which to display his beautiful and imaginative creations. But if the purchase process itself had been littered with troublesome hurdles, those problems were nothing compared with what was to follow.

The building was a typical commercial block from the 1930s, and Cavelti discovered that before he could obtain a permit to convert the street level of the building to accommodate his store, he would have to renovate the building in its entirety: new fire protection, new sprinklers, structural upgrading to earthquake-proof standards, even an internal generator to back up the elevator in case of a power breakdown.

For Cavelti, a novice in the world of construction and restoration, it was a mammoth undertaking. He and Hildegard eventually borrowed a total of $3.4 million to make it possible. They offset some of the costs by agreeing to allow the city to designate the building as a heritage structure, in return receiving permission to add a floor of rental office space at the top, though the rental market collapsed before the conversion was completed, and Cavelti was able to obtain rents amounting to less than half what his initial budget called for. However, the building is now fully leased to long-term tenants, and Cavelti turns away inquiries for space almost daily.

Despite everything, he looks back on the conversion as "a very happy thing to do." It gave him, he says, "the best jewellery-making setup anyone could wish for." The Mayor of Vancouver, Gordon Campbell, was on hand to cut the ribbon at the official opening of the newly refurbished building in 1991; not long after, Cavelti received a City of Vancouver

The elegant simplicity and irresistible flow of this *pavé*-set platinum necklet, discreetly completed by two pear-shaped diamonds, won Cavelti a Diamonds International Award in 1977.

heritage award in recognition of the quality of the restoration. It is typical of this modest man that he kept the building's original name, rejecting initial proposals to call it the Cavelti Building as "too presumptuous."

Today, the building has become an icon of all that Cavelti hoped to do with his life—an icon that all the passing city can see. Painted on the entire face of the building's eastern wall is a mural taken from an old copper engraving. The image depicts a medieval goldsmith at his bench, hammer in hand, bellow for the fire at his feet. Beside him, a colleague is displaying a jewel to an apprentice: passing on the tradition, just as Cavelti has passed on the tradition to his children. Both son Chris and daughter Caroline served short apprenticeships as goldsmiths as well as graduating as gemmologists, and while Caroline now devotes her time to her family, Chris remains busy in the Cavelti business.

The mural embodies the dream that Cavelti had ever since he first saw those illuminated manuscripts in the *Stiftsbibliotek* at the abbey of St. Gallen and captures the spirit of the era with which he feels most at home: the time when persons of skill could devote their lives and their attention to the loving manufacture of the beautiful and enduring object, and take lasting pride in doing so. It is the essence of the story of his life.

Portfolio

The Early Years
From 1957 to the 1960s

Brooch ▪ 18-carat gold, diamonds ▪ 50 mm x 12.5 mm ▪ 1957 ▪ Exhibited at the University of British Columbia craft show in 1957, this was Toni Cavelti's first venture into the use of polished knife-edge gold wire. It is punctuated by diamonds set in delicate, barely visible collets of gold wire. The spiky style, probably influenced by the work of modernist artists active in Vancouver at the time, was to become a familiar look in later Cavelti creations.

Brooch ▪ 18-carat gold, pure gold dust, platinum, diamonds, rubies, sapphires ▪ 35 mm x 35 mm ▪ 1957 ▪ In the 1950s, Toni Cavelti was one of the few jewellers in Vancouver able to show potential clients a painted design of a suggested creation. This cactus plant brooch was commissioned from a painting by Cavelti. The 18-carat gold of the leaves is given a softer texture by a sprinkling of pure gold dust.

Drop earrings ▪ 18-carat gold, platinum, diamonds ▪ 60 mm x 12 mm ▪ circa 1958 ▪ An extremely unusual design for the period, these earrings continued Cavelti's experiments in the use of knife-edge gold wire to make geometric forms. In this case, narrow platinum triangles set with diamonds seem to float over the gold frame.

Necklace with detachable brooch ▪ 18-carat gold, opal, diamonds ▪ 45 mm x 22 mm ▪ circa 1959 ▪ Precious opal, or crystalline silica, is valued for its rich iridescence and the way that the refraction of light by the hardened silica jelly within it creates a changing play of colour, usually red, blue and (as here) green. This brooch, featuring an Australian opal and diamonds set in collets of gold wire, can be detached from the necklace. The gold forms were cut out of a sheet, shaped and individually textured.

Wedding band ▪ 18-carat gold ▪ 1960 ▪ This wedding band was originally two rings for a husband and wife. Later, the two wedding bands were joined to form the one ring shown here. The letters and numerals are 2 mm and 3 mm in height; each was painstakingly cut out and soldered into place.

Brooch-pendant ▪ 18-carat gold, platinum, diamonds ▪ 75 mm x 36 mm ▪ 1960 ▪ The design of this complex structure was probably influenced by the abstract expressionist paintings of Cavelti's artist contemporaries of the time, such as Gordon Smith, Toni Onley and Jack Shadbolt. The deep background grid was formed of square gold wire that Cavelti first crinkled, then stretched (to restore a sense of straightness while retaining a certain "character"). Finally, he applied heat to points in the wire to create a "bubble" effect and superimposed long, seemingly floating rectangles of diamond-bearing platinum.

Brooch ▪ 18-carat gold, diamonds, emeralds, coral ▪ 60 mm x 45 mm ▪ circa 1960 ▪ Created by commission, this fanciful and delicate object looks like something rich and strange plucked from the depths of the ocean. Like the spiky brooches, it was part of Cavelti's attempts to escape from the deadening hand of tradition that had held him in such thrall in his apprentice years in Switzerland. The simple, perfect coral branch is embellished by strands of polished and partially textured round gold wire, decorated by "flowers" of collet-held emeralds and diamonds.

Ring ▪ 18-carat gold, diamonds, tourmaline ▪ 1960 ▪ This traditional, baroque-influenced ring is reminiscent of much of the work that Cavelti undertook as an apprentice. The green tourmaline is supported on scrolls of knife-edge gold wire and embellished with diamonds. The polished, textured leaves were created by the *repoussé* method, in which relief designs are hammered out from the back. The open shank contributes to the ring's sense of airy, effusive decoration.

Brooch-pendant ▪ 18-carat gold, platinum, diamonds, rubies ▪ 50 mm x 35 mm ▪ 1960 ▪ This cross consisting of apparently unconnected blocks is another example of the way the young Cavelti was influenced by the West Coast abstract impressionism that he saw in the work of his artist friends at the New Design Gallery. The diamonds in their platinum squares, and the collet-held rubies, seem to have tumbled by accident into this crucifix form.

Drop earrings ▪ 18-carat white gold, diamonds ▪ 60 mm x 20 mm ▪ 1960 ▪ This complex, apparently haphazard design of gold wire and diamonds called for sophisticated soldering techniques to ensure that none of the contact points in the construction are visible. White gold (known as grey gold, or *or gris* in French) is an alloy of gold, nickel, silver and palladium.

Brooch ▪ 18-carat yellow and white gold, pure gold dust, diamond ▪ 30 mm x 50 mm ▪ circa 1960 ▪ Influences of the new directions in Vancouver art of the late 1950s and early 1960s are discernible in this elegant gold framework. Organic rectangular shapes in white gold, thickly clustered with pure gold dust, float in front of and behind the grid, and a single diamond cut in the brilliant style (whose 58 facets were mathematically devised to produce optimum brilliance) provides an arresting punctuation point.

Brooch-pendant and ring ▪ Brooch: 18-carat gold, diamonds, cameo ▪ 45 mm x 34 mm ▪ 1980 ▪ Ring: 18-carat gold, diamonds ▪ 1960 ▪ Despite the fact that they were created two decades apart, this brooch-pendant and ring make a handsome match. The elegant scrollwork in knife-edge gold wire and the judicious placement of diamonds refer back to the traditional techniques that Cavelti learned as an apprentice in St. Gallen. The style, somewhat rococo, is not dissimilar to the work of the jewellers of the German city of Ulm.

Brooch-pendant ▪ 18-carat white gold, pure gold dust, emeralds, opal ▪ 52 mm x 54 mm ▪ 1960 ▪ An effervescent filigree scribble of white gold wire provides a bed for an oval-shaped Australian opal whose elements of green are picked up and enhanced by a surrounding scattering of collet-held emeralds. The airy vigour of the wirework is softened toward the centre of the piece by clustered sprinkles of pure gold dust.

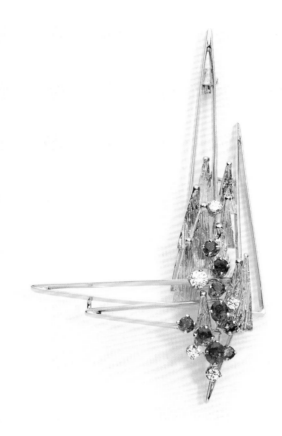

Brooch ▪ 18-carat gold, diamonds, emeralds ▪ 48 mm x 30 mm ▪ circa 1963 ▪ Knife-edge gold wire establishes a vigorous frame in which delicate horizontals give balance and proportion to a strong vertical thrust. Set on and within this frame are precast triangles of textured gold, their bubbled tips softening the work's angularity. Collet-set emeralds and diamonds provide a lush counterpoint to the disciplined form.

Brooch-pendant ▪ 18-carat gold, platinum, diamonds ▪ 40 mm diameter ▪ 1964 ▪ "Any fool can make a complicated piece of jewellery if he knows how to solder," says Toni Cavelti. "Making a simple piece is harder." This celebration of balance and order (the principles at the heart of Cavelti's work) looks simple, but its manufacture was a complex affair. The left half of the pendant is studded with dozens of diamonds in a *pavé* (literally, paved) setting in which multiple stones are set alongside each other in a glittering cobblestone effect. The pendant can be detached to wear as a brooch.

Brooch and earclips ▪ 18-carat gold, pure gold dust, platinum, diamonds ▪ Brooch: 40 mm x 50 mm ▪ 1960 ▪ Earclips: 17.5 mm x 13.6 mm ▪ 1969 ▪ Clearly influenced by the abstract paintings and collages introduced to the Vancouver art scene in the late 1950s by Toni Onley, this brooch reflects the state of spontaneity and excitement in which it was created. It juxtaposes two contrasting gold sheets (one textured, one thickly encrusted with melted-on fine gold dust) against a slightly shaped platinum sheet, its lower corner as jagged as a piece of broken glass, bearing *pavé*-set diamonds. The earclips feature ovals of encrusted gold and convex, and diamond-set platinum forms whose slender, pointed shapes echo the jagged lower corner of the brooch's platinum sheet.

Brooch ▪ 18-carat gold, diamond, South Seas pearl, emeralds ▪ 60 mm x 30 mm ▪ circa 1962 ▪ This tropical bird holding a diamond in its beak is a fanciful design in which textured gold "plumage" and cabochon (rounded and polished) emeralds highlight the unusual appeal of a lustrous South Seas pearl.

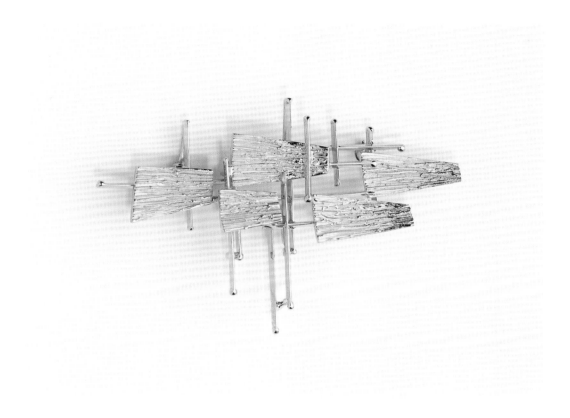

Brooch ▪ 18-carat gold ▪ 60 mm x 40 mm ▪ circa 1960 ▪ Another work whose elegant and balanced composition clearly reflects the influence of the Vancouver creative community of the late 1950s (perhaps, in this case, the organic architecture of Arthur Erickson). This brooch conveys a sense of modern dynamism and speed by allowing slightly concave and apparently airborne textured gold sheets to thrust horizontally out of the restraints of the polished knife-edge gold-wire grid.

The Middle Years

From the 1960s to the Late 1970s

Brooch ▪ Platinum, diamonds ▪ 48 mm x 42 mm ▪ circa 1960 ▪ Suggesting a supernova frozen in mid-explosion in its complex and chaotic cluster of platinum settings, and seemingly held together by nothing more than magnetic force, this circular brooch has a gleam of cold fire that catches the eye from yards away. The outer framework is scattered with old full and brilliant-cut diamonds; at its heart, an old brilliant-cut diamond creates a sense of dense explosion.

Brooch ▪ 18-carat gold, pure gold dust, diamonds ▪ 52 mm x 40 mm ▪ circa 1962 ▪ Judiciously applied clusters of pure gold dust help soften the deliberately jagged and dynamic lines of this starburst design. Collet-set diamonds enhance the impression of lighter-than-air exhilaration.

Brooch ▪ 18-carat gold, pure gold dust ▪ 64 mm x 56 mm ▪ circa 1963 ▪ The airy density of downtown Vancouver during its growth in the 1960s, and the city's contrasts with the spectacular natural landscape in which it is set, inevitably influenced the artists of the period. In this brooch, Cavelti seems to be reflecting the contrasting sensuousness and formality of his surroundings in surfaces that are alternately highly polished and highly textured (sheets of gold on which gold dust has been melted).

Brooch-pendant ▪ 18-carat gold, pure gold dust, aquamarine, diamonds ▪ 65.5 mm x 48 mm ▪ circa 1963 ▪ Meticulous and painstaking scrollwork in 0.8-mm diameter round gold wire lightly dusted with pure gold grain provides an elegant and airy pillow on which to display a spectacular Brazilian aquamarine (which, like the emerald, is a member of the beryl family of minerals). A luxurious scattering of collet-held diamonds subtly enhances the appeal of the pure colouring of the stone.

Pendant ▪ 18-carat gold, pure gold grain, diamonds, pearls ▪ 70 mm x 38 mm ▪ circa 1963 ▪ A roughly circular gold disc, thickly encrusted with gold grain, is contained within an asymmetrical diamond-studded wire frame bearing swinging gold rods surmounted by pearls. The piece is an early example of the way in which Cavelti was to blend references to the primitive with the ultramodern to create art objects whose appeal (and metaphorical freighting) spanned the centuries.

Necklace ▪ 18-carat gold, jade ▪ circa 1975 ▪ This varihued piece of carved jade, as rawly, immediately beautiful as if it had just been wrested from the ground, exemplifies the timelessness of the appeal of precious stones. The chain of fused links of twisted, melted gold accentuates the sense of the elemental.

Brooch-pendant ▪ 18-carat gold, pure gold dust, platinum, diamonds, opal ▪ 56 mm x 43.5 mm ▪ circa 1965 ▪ The intricate star effect of the explosion of knife-edge gold wire, together with the tapering "rays" of diamond-set platinum and scattered sparks of collet-set diamonds around this gorgeously iridescent Australian opal, captures a cosmic moment for eternity. Sprinkled pure gold dust adds to the richness, while delicate soldering and layering give it a lighter-than-air fragility.

Brooch-pendant ▪ 18-carat gold, white and grey cultured pearls ▪ 43 mm x 60 mm ▪ circa 1965 ▪ Looking like the head, perhaps, of some fanciful bird of paradise, this openwork structure of gold wire takes its character and charm from the artful clustering and counterbalancing of the mixed pearls. An interesting sense of dimension is achieved by placing the wires and the pearls at different levels. The mechanics of the piece are so effortlessly hidden that the "bird" appears to be flying.

Ring ▪ 18-carat gold, diamonds ▪ circa 1965 ▪ Despite the sense of solidity conveyed by the cubes in which these diamonds are contained, this ring has an airy, suspended appearance that owes much to the unusual open shank, in which a spring has been incorporated to ensure that the ring stays securely on the finger.

Bracelet ▪ 18-carat gold ▪ 40 mm x 165 mm ▪ 1965 ▪ "Our coliseum bracelet," jokes Cavelti about this arenalike abstraction that evokes the structure of the new Vancouver Public Library just a block away from his downtown salon. This multilayered structure is built from open gold links, cast by the lost wax method; they are lightly textured on the outer surfaces and soldered into this handsome shape that hints not merely at ancient Rome but at primal prehistory.

Brooch ▪ 18-carat gold, pure gold dust, diamonds, tourmaline ▪ 76 mm x 44 mm ▪ circa 1965 ▪ The spiky symmetries of Cavelti's early experiments in abstract line using knife-edge gold wire are softened here by the introduction of a scattering of varisized, collet-set diamonds, a judicious application of fine gold dust and the finely judged placement of a spectacular green tourmaline.

Brooch ▪ 18-carat gold, pure gold dust, platinum, diamonds, emeralds ▪ 22.5 mm x 61.5 mm ▪ 1965 ▪ The influence of the linearity of 1960s Vancouver abstract modernism seems tempered here by the lush orientalism of early twentieth-century designs for the Ballets Russes. Sensuousness and sinuosity play against each other as the freeform diamond-encrusted platinum sheets undulate around the thickly textured gold.

Ring ▪ 18-carat gold, diamonds ▪ circa 1965 ▪ The exuberant imagination of Cavelti's work of the 1960s is beautifully exemplified in this ingenious creation. The floating, diamond-tipped gold tubes, connected by 1-mm diameter
round gold wire, suggest some kind of fanciful molecular structure, an idea reinforced by the cross-strutted,
open shank.

Necklace ▪ 18-carat gold, diamonds, lavender jade, cultured pearls ▪ circa 1965 ▪ At the heart of this clean, classic design, the lavender jade stone is suspended in a casting of gold studded with brilliant-cut diamonds. Six strands of 3-mm diameter cultured pearls, plaited into the necklace, complement the extraordinary warmth and richness of the gemstone.

Necklace ▪ 18-carat gold, pure gold dust, diamonds, pearls ▪ 45 mm diameter ▪ 1965 ▪ Gold's ability to evoke a sense of prehistory is much in evidence here, suggesting perhaps the cracking of some cosmic egg and the spilling forth of an ancient, mysterious beauty. The necklace opens up on a series of invisible hinges.

Brooch ▪ 18-carat gold, platinum, diamonds ▪ 37.5 mm x 67.5 mm ▪ circa 1965 ▪ This abstract design was perhaps inspired by hearing architect Arthur Erickson talk about the qualities of raw concrete as a structural form. Precast and textured gold panels provide an elemental backdrop for diamond-set platinum sheets and a single large collet-set diamond.

Brooch-pendant ▪ 18-carat white gold, diamonds, aquamarine ▪ 56 mm x 46.5 mm ▪ circa 1967 ▪ The scattering of collet-set diamonds and the delicate framework of highly polished 1-mm diameter round wires upon which this exquisite gemstone is mounted throw off a dazzling icy fire. Aquamarine, Brazil's best-known gemstone, ranges through the entire blue spectrum; its chemical composition is identical to that of the emerald.

Brooch-pendant ▪ 18-carat gold, pure gold dust, diamonds, emeralds, South Seas pearl ▪ 55 mm x 41.25 mm ▪ 1967 ▪ South Seas pearls can be round, drop-shaped, pear-shaped, circular or, as here, baroque. The appeal of the baroque pearl lies not only in its soft, satiny lustre but also in its inexact shaping, set off here by the encircling arrangement of claw-set diamonds and Colombian emeralds on a crusted gold form reminiscent of an underwater flower.

Brooch-pendant ▪ 18-carat gold, pure gold dust, diamonds ▪ 60 mm x 40.8 mm ▪ 1968 ▪ This sleek and arresting composition juxtaposes highly polished gold panels, jewel-topped gold wire circles and a cascade of graduated gold spheres against a densely crusted abstract gold form. The interplay of lines and circles gives the design an elegant tension reminiscent of Cubist or Constructivist painting. The brooch is detachable from the necklace of slender gold wire.

Pendant and ring ▪ 18-carat white gold, South Seas pearls, diamonds ▪ Pendant 45 mm x 80 mm ▪ circa 1968 ▪ A tumbling cascade of baguette and brilliant-cut diamonds reaches an emphatic climax in this gleaming, satiny baroque South Seas pearl. The ring features a similar pearl encircled by collet-set, brilliant-cut diamonds.

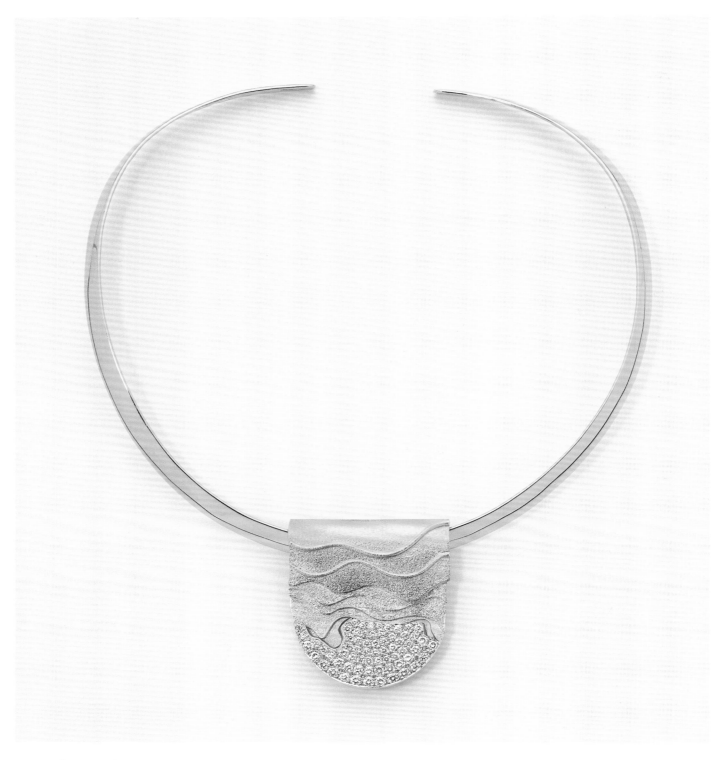

Brooch-pendant ▪ 18-carat gold, platinum, diamonds ▪ 45 mm x 42 mm ▪ 1968 ▪ This detachable pendant suggests a classic shield displaying a decorative coat of arms. Its semicircular platinum shape bears *pavé*-set diamonds, set in a field of textured gold.

Brooch-pendant ▪ 18-carat yellow and white gold, pure gold grain, diamonds ▪ 43 mm x 50 mm ▪ circa 1969 ▪ In its fluid shaping and casual clustering of precious stones, this abstract creation seems to refer back across the centuries to Egyptian or Inca times. However, Toni Cavelti has always been scrupulous in his determination to ensure that his organic forms remain nonspecific, and the piece can be enjoyed simply for the satisfactions of its line and elegant, quietly gleaming beauty. The gold form is densely crusted with fine gold grain, and the brilliant-cut diamonds are set at various levels in collets of white gold.

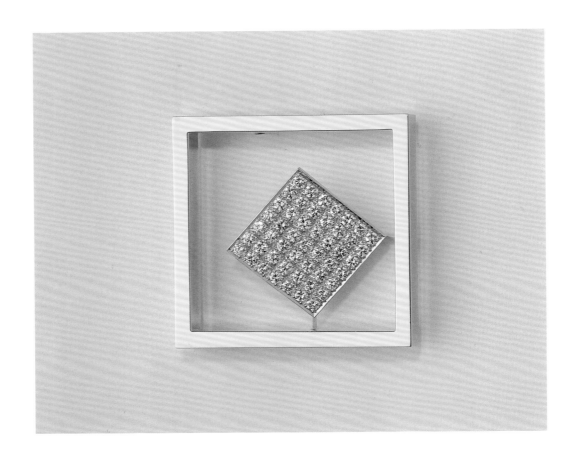

Brooch ▪ 18-carat gold, platinum, diamonds ▪ 40 mm x 40 mm ▪ circa 1970 ▪ The spare, open style of the work of Cavelti's artist friend Gordon Smith in the 1960s may have been an influence here, but the effect is all Cavelti— a highly polished gold square frame setting off a dazzling platinum square of *pavé*-set diamonds.

Ring ▪ 18-carat gold, diamonds ▪ circa 1970 ▪ *Pavé*-set diamonds accentuate highly polished gold cubes on an openwork shank. The tumbling-dice effect looks haphazard, but the positioning was a matter of exact precision and balance to allow the ring to sit well on the wearer's finger.

Brooch-pendant ▪ 18-carat gold, pure gold dust ▪ 65.6 mm x 41.6 mm ▪ 1970 ▪ The symbol for gold, *Au,* derives from the Latin word for gold, *aurum,* meaning "shining dawn." This exercise in controlled design vivacity captures a sense of freshness, counterposing highly polished gold forms with surfaces textured by an overlay of sprinkled gold dust. The vertical severity of the design frame is softened by an artful curving-back of a polished leaf and the playful positioning of the single gold globe, or sun.

Necklace ▪ 18-carat gold, diamonds, emeralds, amethyst ▪ circa 1970 ▪ A lighter-than-air mesh of 0.8-mm diameter round gold wire, supported by a matching flexible chain, is studded with collet-set diamonds and cabochon emeralds to provide a setting of delicacy and charm for the superb amethyst. The most valuable of the quartzes, and once owned exclusively by the nobility and the clergy, the amethyst is said to be a love charm, a sleep inducer and (as indicated by its Greek name, *a-methistos,* which literally means "not inebriated") a protection against the effects of alcohol.

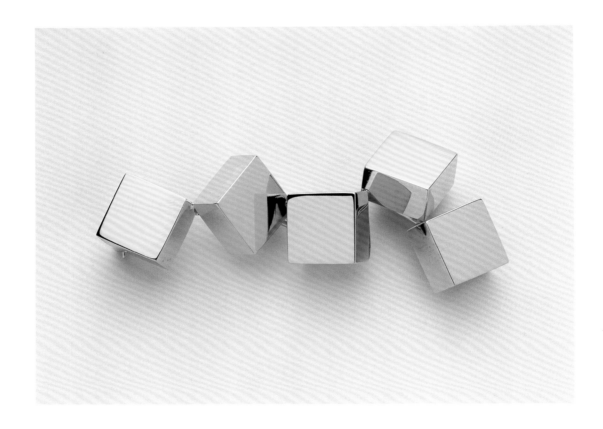

Brooch ▪ 18-carat gold ▪ 25 mm x 60 mm ▪ circa 1970 ▪ This spectacularly simple brooch of irregularly placed, highly polished gold blocks suggests the ultimate abstraction of a child's game, or a three-dimensional rendering of some of the elemental designs of Cavelti's artist friends in 1960s Vancouver.

Necklace with detachable brooch, earclips ▪ 18-carat gold, platinum, diamonds, freshwater pearls, rubellite ▪ Brooch 40 mm x 30 mm ▪ Earclips 22 mm x 19 mm ▪ 1970 ▪ Rubellite is one of the most valuable varieties of the tourmaline, a gemstone whose infinitely graduated spectrum of hues (ranging from colourless through green to pink to red to blue to violet to black) makes it easy to confuse with (and an excellent alternative to) many other stones, among them the ruby, the emerald and the sapphire. This beautiful pink rubellite is set off by a classical, polished gold frame enclosing *pavé*-set diamonds on a platinum base. The delicate colouring of the stone is intensified by the milky gleam of thick strands of freshwater pearls from Lake Biwa in Japan.

Necklace, ring and earclips ▪ 18-carat gold, platinum, diamonds, emeralds ▪ circa 1970-73 ▪ This set was designed and created to display some of the most significant stones to pass through the Cavelti workshop—a group of matched emeralds acquired by Cavelti expressly for this commission from Colombia, traditionally the producer of the world's finest examples of this precious gem. The classical simplicity of the traditional cut of the emeralds—an oblong plateau on the upper surface, intended to bring out the intensity of the green—is echoed in the handsome linear formality of the diamond-set, platinum-lined, polished gold frames.

Ring ▪ 18-carat gold, platinum, diamonds ▪ circa 1972 ▪ This unusual ring, created for a commission, features a shank of textured, partly melted gold strips whose apparently random positioning both echoes the cut of the platinum-held, emerald-cut diamonds and hints at the natural crystal formations in which many precious gemstones are found.

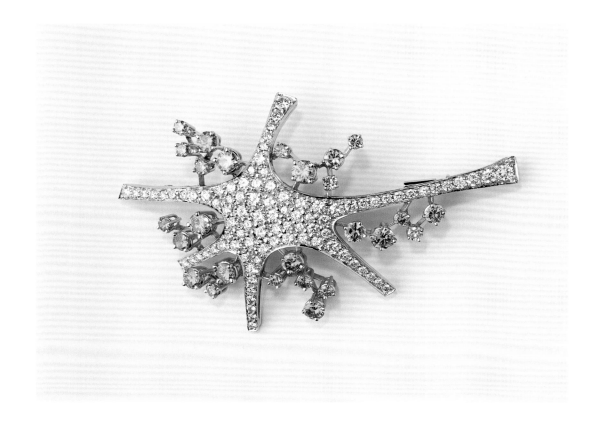

Brooch-pendant ▪ Platinum, white and yellow diamonds ▪ 41.6 mm x 68.8 mm ▪ circa 1973 ▪ Imaginative exuberance and sophisticated structural skills combine here to suspend forever a gleaming splash of sun-flashed water in the micro-second of its happening. *Pavé*-set white diamonds on a freeform platinum base are surrounded by scattered yellow diamonds set in collets to give a lively sense of spray.

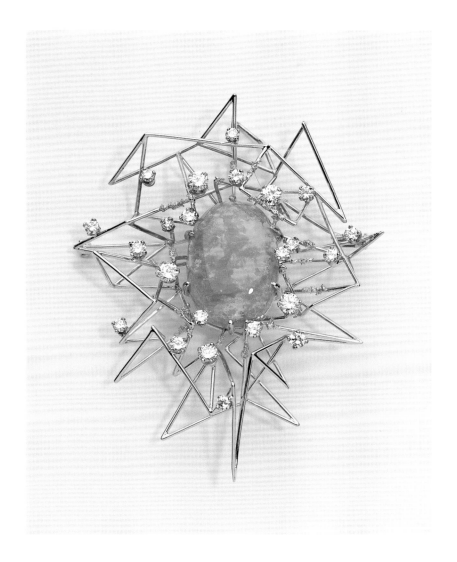

Brooch-pendant ▪ 18-carat gold, pure gold dust, diamonds, opal ▪ 63.75 mm x 48.75 mm ▪ circa 1975 ▪ Most of the world's supply of gem-quality opal comes from Australia, where this iridescent, green-blue stone was mined. The starburst angularity of the framework of round gold wire is softened by the judicious application of melted pure gold dust; brilliant-cut diamonds set in collets add sparkle to the opal's warmth and lustre. Note the clever manner in which the vertical gold spur at the bottom of the piece gives it balance.

Necklace ▪ 18-carat yellow and white gold, diamonds, emeralds ▪ circa 1975 ▪ The glorious autumnal warmth of this necklace comes from the interplay between the evocative texturing of the precast gold leaf forms and the profusion of rounded (cabochon) emeralds. A scattering of collet-set diamonds and the delicacy of the linking gold threads contribute to a sense of the spontaneous discovery of random natural beauty.

Ring ▪ 18-carat gold, platinum, diamonds ▪ circa 1975 ▪ This classic Cavelti ring features a split gold shank sur-mounted by a single brilliant-cut diamond supported by four platinum claws that are themselves *pavé*-set with diamonds.

Necklace ▪ 18-carat gold, platinum, diamonds ▪ circa 1975 ▪ The dogwood-flower design is accentuated by the use of brilliant-cut cinnamon-coloured diamonds at the heart of each set of five platinum "petals" *pavé*-set in brilliant-cut white diamonds. Textured "leaves" in gold complete the statement. Both the brooch and the earclips may be detached.

Necklace ▪ 18-carat gold, platinum, pearls, tanzanite ▪ 1975 ▪ Tanzanite takes its name from the African country of Tanzania, where it was first discovered in 1967. The crystals are found in colours ranging from yellow-green and brown to blue, violet and the blue-purple seen here. This cushion-shaped, faceted tanzanite is set on a classic shield shape of polished gold and appears to be suspended from a thick rope of brilliant-cut diamonds, *pavé*-set on platinum. The brooch is detachable from the multistranded necklace of cultured pearls from Lake Biwa.

Necklace, ring and drop earrings ▪ Platinum, diamonds, sapphires ▪ 1975-78 ▪ The world supply of sapphires has become so restricted that this unique setting of extremely fine matched oval, cushion- and pear-shaped sapphires would be difficult to replicate today. Created as a commission, this *parure,* or suite, sets the deep, icy beauty of the gemstones against a cool and lustrous backdrop of clustered diamonds and shimmering platinum.

Necklace and ring ▪ 18-carat gold, platinum, diamonds, pearls, sapphires ▪ circa 1975 ▪ The star sapphire is among the most prized of gemstones. Its six-rayed star effect, known as asterism, is caused by the reflection of light by needlelike foreign particles within the stone. The velvety richness of these spectacular examples is accentuated in the necklace by a platinum setting of *pavé*-set diamonds and a diamond-punctuated strand of milky pearls, and in the ring by an encirclement of bezel-set diamonds.

Pendant ▪ 18-carat gold, pure gold dust ▪ 55 mm x 50 mm ▪ circa 1975 ▪ As handsome and imposing as an amulet from ancient Egypt or Peru, as clean and direct in its design as a piece of twentieth-century sculpture, this badge-shaped gold pendant marries three distinct surface textures in a singing harmony of gleaming, glinting form.

Brooch-pendant ▪ 18-carat gold, pure gold dust, platinum, diamonds ▪ 57.6 mm x 47.7 mm ▪ 1975 ▪ The crusted gold surface of the egg of creation has broken apart, revealing its diamond-studded inner layer, and out spills the world's first bounty: a profusion of pear-shaped, baguette and brilliant-cut diamonds on an artful frame of platinum forms and collets.

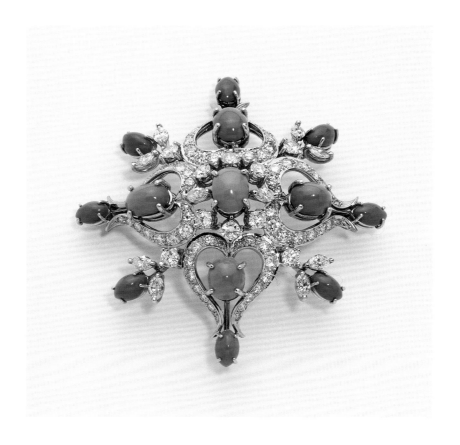

Brooch-pendant ▪ 18-carat white gold, diamonds, turquoise ▪ 60 mm x 60 mm ▪ circa 1975 ▪ While it is not suitable for cutting and faceting into a brilliant gem, the opaque turquoise is much prized for its milky lustre. In this commissioned creation, the turquoise comes into its own: a single stone is encircled by four heart-shaped white gold forms studded with brilliant-cut diamonds, each form set with turquoises at its centre and tip. The entire structure is decorated with diamond sprays that have turquoises as their "flowers."

Pendant and earrings ▪ 18-carat white gold, diamonds, sapphires ▪ circa 1978 ▪ This classical setting of rare and spectacular sapphires has a splendid elegance of style that would not have disgraced the Romanoff court. Starburst sprays of collet-set, full-cut diamonds throw rings of icy fire around the sapphires. A member of the corundum mineral species (the hardest substance after diamond), the sapphire derives its colouring from traces of iron and titanium; the stones can be polished to a high gloss, as here, to make full use of the effect of their deep, rich blues.

Necklace ▪ 18-carat gold, diamonds, opal ▪ circa 1978 ▪ Sensuously curved and moulded gold shapes created by the lost wax technique give an air of prehistory to this gorgeously tactile setting of a freeform Australian opal. In its delicate interplay of twinkling colours, the opal's prismatic beauty has been compared to the *aurora australis,* or "southern lights," of Antarctica. Its milky appearance is due to multitudinous tiny cracks in its surface.

Brooch-pendant ▪ 18-carat gold, platinum, diamonds ▪ 45 mm x 45 mm ▪ 1978 ▪ Commissioned as a gift for a customer's wife, this handsome brooch-pendant sets a geometric platinum framework of initials spelled out in brilliant- and baguette-cut diamonds within a half-tube frame of polished gold. Platinum corner-hoops complete the impression of dignified harmony.

The Later Years

From 1980 to the Present

Brooch and drop earrings ▪ 18-carat yellow and white gold, diamonds, rubies, sapphire, moonstones ▪ Brooch 52 mm x 43.2 mm ▪ circa 1980 ▪ The blue-tinged milky lustre of the moonstone that forms the body of this "insect" brooch is caused by light refraction from the interior of the stone. It plays artfully against the dark blue of the pear-shaped sapphire that forms the insect's head. Cabochon rubies are its eyes.

Ring ▪ 18-carat gold, diamonds ▪ circa 1980 ▪ Blocks of polished gold tumble around collet-set diamonds on a solid, polished gold shank. Sleek and stylish, simple yet substantial, this is a classic Cavelti design from the 1980s.

Brooch ▪ 18-carat gold, pure gold dust, opal ▪ 45 mm x 35 mm ▪ 1980 ▪ An opal of this quality, purity and iridescence is a rarity today. Created as a commission, this brooch displays the pear-shaped Australian opal's dazzling greens and blues in the clasp of a broad, free-form ribbon of gold that is densely encrusted with pure gold dust.

Necklace ▪ 18-carat gold, diamonds, emeralds, carved emerald ▪ circa 1980 ▪ The cabochon emerald around which this superb piece was built was carved in India and weighs more than 100 carats (1 carat equals 200 milligrams). Its textured gold setting bears groupings of *pavé*-set diamonds. The triple-stranded necklace by which the stone is supported consists of strings of emeralds alternating with small gold spheres.

Necklace and ring ▪ 18-carat white gold, diamonds, tourmalines ▪ Necklace 40 cm long approx. ▪ 1988 ▪
A spectacular specimen of the rare blue (indicolite) tourmaline, also mistakenly known as Brazilian sapphire, is
displayed here in a rampant profusion of worked and polished white gold wire studded with collet-set, brilliant-
cut diamonds. The flat-topped, side-canted emerald cut favoured for inclusion-free stones such as this one takes
optimum advantage of its transparent hue. The matching ring sets an oval-faceted indicolite tourmaline in a circle of
collet-set diamonds.

Bracelet and brooch-pendant ▪ 18-carat gold, platinum, diamonds ▪ Bracelet 25 mm x 60 mm ▪ circa 1980 ▪ Brooch-pendant 60 mm x 50 mm ▪ circa 1982 ▪ In terms of the intricate workmanship and the quality of their stones, these elaborate, commissioned fabrications on the theme of the butterfly more than hint at the style of the great Russian *ateliers* of the late nineteenth century. At the heart of the bracelet is a superb diamond cut in the marquise style (an elaborately faceted pointed oval or boat shape). Smaller marquise-cut and baguette-cut diamonds are offset by *pavé*-set, brilliant-cut diamonds in the "wings" of the butterfly and adorn the intricate gold scrollwork of the bracelet. The "body" of the brooch is a polished oval (faceted) diamond of natural yellow colour, embellished by brilliant-cut diamonds *pavé*-set on platinum on a gold wire frame; two baguette-cut diamonds provide brilliant emphasis.

Necklace with detachable centrepiece ▪ 18-carat gold, diamonds, emeralds, cultured pearls, sapphire ▪ Centrepiece 35 mm x 30 mm ▪ circa 1980 ▪ Setting off the rich and shimmering blue of the central sapphire is an encircling cluster of marquise-cut emeralds and brilliant-cut diamonds set in gold collets. The first use of sapphires in jewellery dates back to the early Roman Empire, when the hardest carbon-based stones were used in uncut but polished form. In medieval times, sapphires were believed to help the wearer lead a pure life and were set in rings for the clergy.

Necklace with detachable centrepiece ▪ 18-carat gold, platinum, diamonds, cultured pearls, emerald ▪ Centrepiece 35 mm x 30 mm ▪ circa 1983 ▪ Keshi pearls are tiny, formed as a by-product in the creation of cultured pearls. The beautiful silky sheen of hundreds of Keshi pearls throws an aura of luxury and calm around the formal dazzle of this rare Colombian emerald displayed in a classic platinum-mounted, *pavé*-set diamond framework. The emerald was acquired by Cavelti for a regular customer he bumped into at an airport. "Where are you going?" asked the customer. Cavelti said he was on his way to a gem exhibition in the U.S. "Pick me up a great emerald for my wife," said the customer.

Necklace, earclips and ring ▪ Platinum, diamonds, rubies ▪ circa 1982 ▪ This magnificent *parure* is built around a set of gorgeous rubies acquired by Cavelti on a trip to the Orient. They are simply cut and set, with the icy sparkle and elegant opulence of platinum and diamonds creating a brilliant contrast for the rich, deep warmth of the rubies.

Pendant on handmade chain ▪ 18-carat gold ▪ Pendant 50 mm diameter ▪ Chain 40 cm long ▪ circa 1984 ▪ Two numerals are present but are barely recognizable in this commission. Cavelti met the challenge of turning a commemorative memento into an object of art by subtly stretching and interweaving the characters into what appears to be a refined piece of decorative linear abstraction.

Necklace, pendant, drop earrings and ring ▪ 18-carat gold, diamonds, cultured pearls, pink topaz ▪ circa 1985 ▪ Pink topaz has always been one of the rarest of the topazes. Stones of the quality of this suite are virtually unobtainable today, so it is perhaps ironic that the topaz is traditionally believed to eradicate envy. This bold, almost exclamatory setting uses precast "tongs" of polished gold and *pavé*-set diamonds to clasp the magnificent pendant stone in a celebratory embrace. The depth and richness of the gem's transparent, lustrous hue is mirrored in the earrings and the simple, spectacular ring. Seven strands of cultured pearls are brought together in a clasp of diamond-encrusted polished gold to complete the effect of exuberance and joy.

Necklace with detachable brooch ▪ 18-carat white gold, platinum, diamonds, tourmaline ▪ Brooch 40 mm x 35 mm ▪ 1985 ▪ Twentieth-century flourishes provide an up-to-date twist on this classic *pavé*-set diamond framework for a gorgeous oval-shaped indicolite tourmaline. The tourmaline is found in the greatest range of colours of any gem, often combining two or three colours in the same stone.

Necklace ▪ 18-carat white gold, diamonds, sapphires ▪ circa 1985 ▪ Milky velvet cabochon-cut sapphires displaying a six-pointed star effect intermingle with sapphires faceted and polished to take maximum advantage of their rich blue depths. Brilliant-cut diamonds twinkle amid this cosmic splendour.

Earclips and ring ▪ Platinum, diamonds, sapphires ▪ Earclips 18 mm x 15 mm ▪ circa 1985 ▪ The settings for each of the tapered baguette diamonds that encircle these deep blue faceted sapphires were meticulously fashioned by hand. They suggest starbursts in deep space, an effect intensified by the dark depths of their coloration.

Necklace ▪ 18-carat gold, cultured pearls ▪ circa 1985 ▪ Molten and textured gold strips give this unusual neck adornment an air of prehistory. The scattered profusion of cultured pearls seems to float without visible means of support, like a moon's clustered stars in a timeless otherworld.

Pendant ▪ 18-carat gold, diamonds, sapphires, rubies, emerald ▪ 31 mm x 27 mm ▪ circa 1985 ▪ Over the years, Cavelti has developed a *clientèle* that is both discriminating and trusting. This piece is one of several that were commissioned by a client who simply requested "something special." It is both special and spectacular—with classic simplicity the key to its success. On a gold base, octagonal oblong settings of rubies, emeralds and brilliant-cut diamonds provide a natural frame for the traditional oblong cut of the Colombian emerald that is the piece's *raison d'être*.

Necklace and pendant ▪ 18-carat gold, platinum, diamonds, emeralds, sapphires, rubellite ▪ circa 1986 ▪
Absolutely flawless rubellites are extremely rare. This large, beautiful pear-shaped rubellite in highly prized pigeon's-blood red is set on a platinum base *pavé*-set with diamonds and studded with collet-set sapphires and emeralds. It is suspended on a flexible chain of knitted, wrought gold wire sprinkled with collet-set diamonds.

Necklace with detachable centrepiece • 18-carat gold, platinum, diamonds, sapphires, lapis lazuli, rubellite • Centrepiece 42 mm x 37.5 mm • circa 1988 • The "sapphire" of ancient times, lapis lazuli was once used widely in mosaics and ground to powder to function as a rich pigment for paint. This string of highly polished lapis beads supports an imposing setting of a splendid cabochon rubellite held within platinum arms that are *pavé*-set with diamonds and joined by a gold hoop set with square sapphires.

Necklace ▪ 18-carat gold, platinum, diamond, pearls ▪ Centrepiece 25 mm x 60 mm ▪ circa 1988 ▪ Never content merely to replicate the formal ostentation of European jewellery of the late nineteenth and early twentieth century, Toni Cavelti has continually explored ways to integrate sensuality and informality into his designs in a way that is both tasteful and timeless. The sensuous curves of this slightly textured gold centrepiece, created by the lost wax casting technique, are beautifully enhanced by the milky soft rope of Lake Biwa pearls. The platinum-set marquise-cut diamond nestled in the central gold form adds a dazzling contrast.

Brooch-pendant ▪ 18-carat gold, platinum, diamonds ▪ 40 mm x 70 mm ▪ circa 1988 ▪ "You used to do wonderful things with gold sticks," a customer said to Toni Cavelti one day in 1988. "Why don't you do them any more?" So Cavelti made him this back-to-beginnings "sticky brooch": textured and polished rectangular 1.2-mm diameter gold wire, with 107 diamonds *pavé*-set on platinum bars.

Necklace, earrings and ring ▪ 18-carat gold, platinum, diamonds, emeralds, aquamarines ▪ circa 1988 ▪ Four rare and immaculate African aquamarines are teamed in this magnificent commissioned *parure* with square Colombian emeralds (the two gemstones are chemically identical) and *pavé*-set diamonds. The diamond-encircled, pear-shaped pendant is detachable.

Brooch-pendant ▪ 18-carat gold, diamond, rosewood ▪ 35 mm x 45 mm ▪ circa 1988 ▪ A dark rosewood becomes a setting of velvety black night for this scattered galaxy of diamond "stars" set in gold collets—a compelling example of Cavelti's gift for fashioning the simplest of designs into a spectacular effect.

Necklace ▪ 18-carat gold, platinum, diamonds, lapis lazuli ▪ circa 1988 ▪ Although lapis lazuli, like turquoise and jade, belongs to a group of gemstones that are found in mass form, rather than crystal form, and are therefore unsuitable for cutting into transparent or translucent gems, it is nevertheless a stone of great beauty, particularly when it is polished and rounded, cabochon-style. This tasteful design displays a gorgeous Afghanistan lapis stone in an elegant surround of diamonds *pavé*-set in platinum in slender gold-framed triangles.

Pendant, bracelet, earclips and ring ▪ 18-carat gold, platinum, diamonds, tanzanites ▪ Pendant 40 mm x 35 mm ▪ Bracelet 18 mm x 170 mm ▪ Earclips 25 mm x 20 mm ▪ 1988 ▪ This complex and highly decorative suite echoes the formal styles and skills of Cavelti's apprenticeship in Switzerland. Meticulous working in gold and diamonds (brilliant-cut and *pavé*-set in platinum around the principal stones, and baguette-cut to decorate the bracelet's links) sets off the imposing power and rich blues of the sapphirelike tanzanites.

Necklace, bracelet and drop earrings ▪ 18-carat gold, diamond ▪ 1988 ▪ The great skill involved in creating this ecstatic, lyrical suite lies in its apparent spontaneity. The premelted 1-mm diameter round gold wire

appears to have been scribbled and twisted into place in the inspiration of a moment. The necklace hinges are invisible, giving the ensemble a lighter-than-air appearance.

Necklet ▪ 18-carat gold, platinum, diamonds ▪ 1988 ▪ An elegantly proportioned curve of slender hammered and polished gold culminates in a dazzling, platinum-set marquise-cut diamond. What is notable here, in addition to the unerring taste, is the way Cavelti has solved two problems through the positioning of a single baguette-cut diamond. Without detracting from the solitary glory of the principal stone, the platinum-set baguette serves both as a design element, establishing a satisfying unity to the flow of the curving gold, and, more practically, as a disguise for the necklet's hidden clasp.

Brooch ▪ 18-carat gold, platinum, diamonds ▪ 74 mm x 40 mm ▪ 1989 ▪ A sense of quiet joy suffuses this dancing ribbon of polished gold edged with platinum-set diamonds.

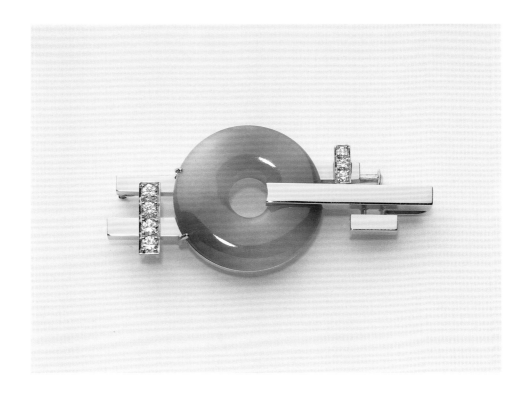

Brooch ▪ 18-carat gold, diamonds, platinum, jade ▪ 26.4 mm x 54.4 mm ▪ circa 1990 ▪ Looking like some ornate and fanciful key to earthly delights, this brooch features a perfect circle of jade suspended in an arrangement of horizontal gold bars punctuated by vertical bars of diamond-set platinum.

Brooch ▪ 18-carat gold, platinum, diamonds ▪ 28 mm x 45 mm ▪ 1990 ▪ Diamonds *pavé*-set in platinum on beautifully flowing loops and ribbons of polished gold give a dazzling richness to this classic bow ribbon brooch. Platinum-set baguette-cut diamonds provide the central accent.

Necklace with pendant ▪ 20-carat gold ▪ 1990 ▪ This unusual commission was fashioned from approximately 20 Spanish coins, melted down and recast by the lost wax method into this heritage pendant. The engraved family crest of the commissioning client can be seen at the centre of the pendant; the leafy texturing conveys the idea of the family's continuity through the passing years.

Brooch-pendant ▪ 18-carat yellow and white gold, diamonds, tourmaline ▪ 60 mm x 50 mm ▪ 1990 ▪ A heaped unspooling of narrow, polished, knife-edge gold ribbon sprinkled with claw-set, brilliant-cut diamonds provides a richly textured bed for the breathtaking transparency and colouring of this rare, shimmering indicolite tourmaline.

Necklace with interchangeable pendants, drop earrings ▪ 18-carat gold, platinum, diamonds, emerald, tourmalines ▪ circa 1990 ▪ This intricately constructed necklace of polished gold and sheets of diamonds *pavé*-set in platinum, with accents of baguette-cut and brilliant-cut diamonds, is a handsome adornment in its own right.

However, the full *parure* also includes two detachable, interchangeable pendants. One pendant is a gold-framed, heart-shaped, cabochon-cut pink tourmaline, or rubellite, and has matching teardrop-shaped earrings. The other pendant is a classically refined Cavelti setting of a square emerald in *pavé*-set diamonds.

Necklace, earrings and ring ▪ 18-carat gold, diamonds, black Tahitian pearls ▪ circa 1990 ▪ The black pearls of the South Pacific are comparative newcomers to the world of fine jewellery. Their colouring ranges from blue-green to silver-grey; their satiny lustre and sheen is due not to polishing (polishing could damage their relatively soft surface) but to the refraction and reflection of light on the multiple layers of nacreous material that make up the pearl itself. These splendid examples of Tahiti's treasures are set off by clusters of triangular blocks of gold set with triangular-cut diamonds.

Necklet ▪ 18-carat gold, platinum, diamonds, emeralds, sapphires, rubies ▪ 42 cm long ▪ 1991 ▪ An unusual digression from Toni Cavelti's more familiar styles and designs, this delicately detailed necklet of fine tubular gold links displays nine polychromatic gold sleeves, each studded with precious gems and banded at their ends by diamonds *pavé*-set in platinum.

Brooch ▪ 18-carat gold, pure gold grain, tourmalines ▪ 20 mm x 63 mm ▪ 1992 ▪ The so-called "watermelon" tourmaline is a particularly striking example of the way the tourmaline can display a variety of hues within a single stone. These "watermelon" tourmalines are cut on a line perpendicular to the crystal's main axis in order to display the way the concentric colouring changes from dusky pink at the centre to a rich green on the outer layers. A simple lightning bolt of gold dusted with pure gold grain supports and unifies these unusual stones.

Drop earrings ▪ 18-carat gold, diamonds, tourmalines ▪ 60 mm x 25 mm ▪ 1992 ▪ Transparent "watermelon" tourmalines in pink and green are set in textured gold frames with dangling diamond tassels in this commissioned set. The design makes veiled references to jewellery of the baroque and rococo eras, without ever losing touch with its modern origins.

Necklace ▪ 18-carat gold, platinum, diamonds, coin ▪ Centrepiece 30 mm diameter ▪ 1993 ▪ Asked by a customer to provide a suitable setting for a Roman coin, Cavelti took elements of the coin's design and incorporated them into his own design for the textured, medallionlike frame, created in gold by the lost wax process. A discreet bridge of diamonds *pavé*-set in platinum joins the centrepiece to a finely woven gold chain that hints at the enduring splendours of empire.

Bangle bracelet ▪ 18-carat gold, diamonds ▪ 65 mm diameter x 25 mm ▪ 1992 ▪ The trick to the successful manufacture of this evocative lost-wax casting lay in the speed with which the original wax sheeting was crumpled while it was still warm. Claw-set diamonds nestle in the depressions and are clustered on the surfaces, creating an impression of sumptuous antiquity.

Necklace and drop earrings ▪ 18-carat yellow and white gold ▪ 1992 ▪ The customer ordering this commission specifically requested that the piece contain no gemstones. Cavelti responded with a highly contemporary design that nonetheless looks back, in its harmonious simplicity, to the ornaments of antiquity. Brush-finished hexagons of varying sizes are juxtaposed against diamond shapes in white gold.

Pendant ▪ 18-carat gold, platinum, diamonds, ruby, silver coin ▪ 45 mm x 40 mm ▪ 1992 ▪ As if to demonstrate the unbroken connection between goldsmiths of modern times and the tradition of jewellery that has endured since earliest human society, this Roman silver coin floats within a shield-shaped framework of polished, precast gold. Subtly emphasizing the implicit message of timeless worth and authority is a gold-set cabochon ruby and an inlaid panel bearing diamonds *pavé*-set in platinum, all on a substantial gold-link chain.

Pendant ▪ 18-carat gold, platinum, diamonds, ruby ▪ 33.6 mm x 21.6 mm ▪ 1993 ▪ One of the most important stones to be handled in the Cavelti workshops, this shimmering ruby, weighing more than 5 carats, was acquired in Thailand and has a rich, typically Thai darkness of hue. It is encircled by marquise-cut and brilliant-cut diamonds; square-cut diamonds decorate the platinum loop.

Necklace ▪ 18-carat gold, platinum, diamonds, tanzanite ▪ 1993 ▪ Twenty-seven invisibly hinged open gold ovals lined with brilliant-cut diamonds set in platinum form a delicate embrace for this elegant and tasteful setting of a faceted, cushion-cut tanzanite; its rich blue, surrounded as it is by starry diamonds, suggests eternal night.

Brooch ▪ 18-carat gold, platinum, diamonds ▪ 36.8 mm x 47.2 mm ▪ 1994 ▪ Created as a Christmas order, this angel brooch displays a number of goldsmithing techniques. The main shape was created by the *cire perdue* (lost wax) process. The arms, hands, head and trumpet were fabricated from gold sheet, shaped and textured. The hair was created in a manner similar to wig-making: tiny holes approximately 0.5 mm in diameter were drilled, and into these were soldered strands of round, slightly crinkled gold wire, styled to give a "flying" effect. Finally, a platinum ribbon was shaped and set with 1-point (100th of a carat), 1.5-mm diameter full-cut diamonds.

Brooch-pendant ▪ 18-carat gold, platinum, diamonds, ruby ▪ 45 mm x 54 mm ▪ 1994 ▪ The jeweller's fascination with the elemental origins of the materials with which he works is often visible in Toni Cavelti's creations. The texturing of this lost wax gold casting brings to mind a stream-bed in a cavern deep inside a jewel-rich layer of the earth's surface, revealing a narrow seam of platinum-set diamonds and a single cabochon ruby.

Necklace with detachable pendant, earclips and ring ▪ 18-carat gold, platinum, diamonds ▪ 1993-94 ▪
This highly ornamental *parure* is an unabashed celebration of the unrivalled charms of the diamond, not only the
hardest substance known but also one of the most valued. The diamond is a crystalline form of carbon and reg-
isters 10 on Friedrich Mohs's scale of hardness of minerals; talc is the softest, registering 1. It is prized for its
adamantine lustre and for its unique qualities of refraction and dispersion, which allow the cut gem to separate
and throw back with dazzling brilliance and purity the various colours of the light that enters it. The focal points of

this complex creation, which took many months to complete, are the four principal stones. On the ring, a 6.5-carat oval-cut diamond surmounts a shank set with baguette-cut stones. The 21-link necklace, invisibly hinged, displays a profusion of brilliant- and baguette-cut stones, culminating in a spectacular pendant featuring a superb oval-shaped diamond in *pavé*-set brilliant-cut diamonds in a bed of platinum. Earclips matching the pendant complete this breathtaking suite.

Pair of brooch-pendants ▪ 18-carat gold, diamonds, sapphires ▪ 35 mm x 35 mm ▪ 1993 ▪ 18-carat gold, diamonds, tourmalines, sapphires ▪ 40 mm x 42 mm ▪ 1995 ▪ These two charming matched baskets of stone "flowers" demonstrate the significant difference in colour intensity between the sapphire (a corundum crystal) and the tourmaline (a borosilicate). The familiar brilliant blue sapphire is supplemented here by the intense hues of the less well-known yellow, green and pink sapphires. The colours in the tourmaline basket are more pastel, giving a sense of the astonishing range and transparency of this multihued gemstone. In each basket, a scattering of collet-set diamonds adds a brilliant accent.

Necklace, earrings and ring ▪ 18-carat gold, platinum, diamonds, sapphires, tourmalines ▪ 1994 ▪ These tri-angular rubellites, cabochon-cut in a modified pyramid form, are products of the Himalaya Mine at Mesa Grande in California. Their delicate colouring and sensitive response to light are given an artfully simple classical setting in which gold-set circular sapphires are suspended from platinum bars bearing *pavé*-set diamonds. The earrings and ring offer subtle variants on the basic design.

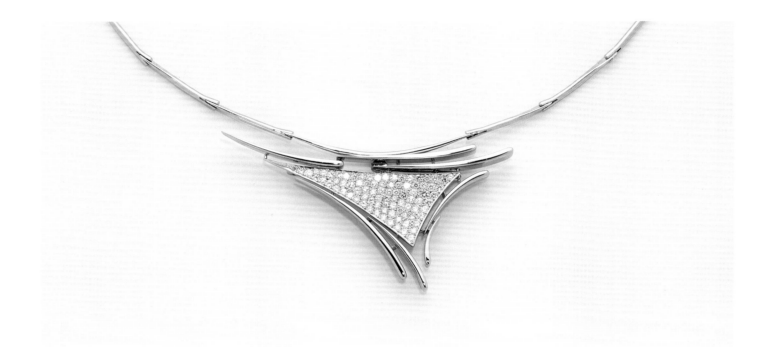

Necklace with detachable brooch-pendant ▪ 18-carat white gold, platinum, diamonds ▪ Necklace 50 cm long ▪ Brooch 36 mm x 72 mm ▪ 1995 ▪ The sleek, chic lines of this elegant modernist abstraction demonstrate that the materials and techniques of the ancient art of the master jeweller remain constantly adaptable. A flying triangle of diamonds *pavé*-set in platinum is flanked by free-form white gold bars whose ardent curves suggest irresistible motion.